BLUEPRINTS

Topics
Key Stage 1

Jim Fitzsimmons

Rhona Whiteford

Stanley Thornes (Publishers) Ltd

Do you receive BLUEPRINTS NEWS?

Blueprints is an expanding series of practical teacher's ideas books and photocopiable resources for use in primary schools. Books are available for separate infant and junior age ranges for every core and foundation subject, as well as for an ever widening range of other primary teaching needs. These include **Blueprints Primary English** books and **Blueprints Resource Banks**. **Blueprints** are carefully structured around the demands of National Curriculum in England and Wales, but are used successfully by schools and teachers in Scotland, Northern Ireland and elsewhere.

Blueprints provide:
- *Total curriculum coverage*
- *Hundreds of practical ideas*
- *Books specifically for the age range you teach*
- *Flexible resources for the whole school or for individual teachers*
- *Excellent photocopiable sheets – ideal for assessment and children's work profiles*
- *Supreme value.*

Books may be bought by credit card over the telephone and information obtained on **(01242) 577944**. Alternatively, photocopy and return this **FREEPOST** form to receive **Blueprints News**, our regular update on all new and existing titles. You may also like to add the name of a friend who would be interested in being on the mailing list.

Please add my name to the **BLUEPRINTS NEWS** mailing list.

Mr/Mrs/Miss/Ms _____

Home address _____

_____ Postcode _____

School address _____

_____ Postcode _____

Please also send **BLUEPRINTS NEWS** to:

Mr/Mrs/Miss/Ms _____

Address _____

_____ Postcode _____

To: Marketing Services Dept., Stanley Thornes Ltd, FREEPOST (GR 782), Cheltenham, GL50 1BR

First published in 1993 by:
Stanley Thornes (Publishers) Ltd
Ellenborough House
Wellington Street
CHELTENHAM GL50 1YW

Reprinted 1993, 1995

A catalogue record for this book is available from the British Library.

ISBN 0 7487 1582 7

Typeset by Tech-Set, Gateshead, Tyne & Wear.
Printed and bound in Great Britain.

CONTENTS

INTRODUCTION

Blueprints Topics Key Stage 1 is a teacher resource book for topic work in the 5 to 7 age group. It consists of an extensive structured bank of ideas for 8 topics and 56 copymaster sheets. The book is structured around the demands of National Curriculum, but may be used just as successfully by schools not following National Curriculum courses. All the topics are cross-curricular referenced to National Curriculum attainment targets to help with your curriculum planning. The aim of *Blueprints Topics* is to provide you with a resource which will enable you to meet the growing need for properly planned and focussed topic work with clear learning objectives and coherent activities related to National Curriculum.

With this in mind you will find that each of the 8 topics in this book provides the following resources:

- a topic web that maps out the topic across the curriculum and gives an indication of attainment targets covered;

- a list of basic concepts that the topic introduces;

- seven practical activity sheets for pupil use. These can form the basis of individual topic works or classroom displays.

Although they are all carefully structured around National Curriculum, it has been felt appropriate with Key Stage 1 to allow the topics to be fully cross-curricular. Each one contains all the elements of the National Curriculum's core and foundation subjects, relevant to the particular age groups.

The topics are loosely graded at three levels of difficulty to meet the needs of the first three years of school. Loosely, the first three topics are for reception classes, the second three for middle infants and the final two for top infants. The ideas for work in each topic are designed to fit in with general expectations of attainment for the age group and are based on the authors' wide experience of teaching these age groups. However, the topics do represent a continuum of difficulty and no attempt has been made formally to grade them; you will find that they can be fitted to the needs of your own individual children and situation.

Blueprints Topics Key Stage 1 provides ideas for approaching topics from many different angles and allows the teacher and children to choose their own starting points. It does not attempt to replace the many excellent individual subject topic books available but is designed to help the teacher to plan an overall strategy. This means that the topics may be studied in their entirety, or single subject areas may be studied in isolation. The cross-curricular references are available when required to enable you to integrate the topics into your National Curriculum planning.

Other books in this series include *Blueprints Topics 5–8*, *Blueprints Writing* and *Blueprints Assemblies*. Many of the ideas, activities and photocopiable pages in these books can be used to complement the topics in this book.

TOYS

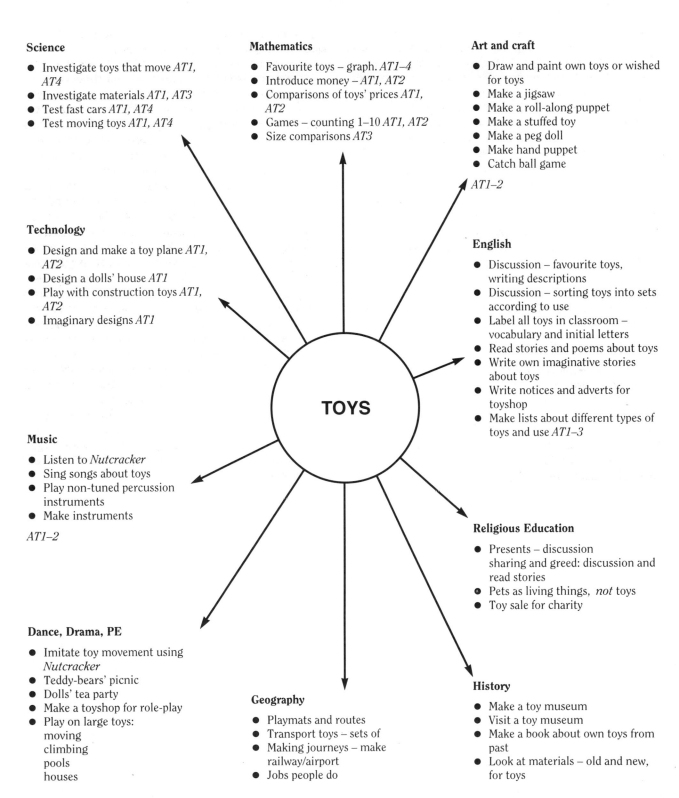

Science

- Investigate toys that move *AT1, AT4*
- Investigate materials *AT1, AT3*
- Test fast cars *AT1, AT4*
- Test moving toys *AT1, AT4*

Technology

- Design and make a toy plane *AT1, AT2*
- Design a dolls' house *AT1*
- Play with construction toys *AT1, AT2*
- Imaginary designs *AT1*

Music

- Listen to *Nutcracker*
- Sing songs about toys
- Play non-tuned percussion instruments
- Make instruments

AT1–2

Dance, Drama, PE

- Imitate toy movement using *Nutcracker*
- Teddy-bears' picnic
- Dolls' tea party
- Make a toyshop for role-play
- Play on large toys:
  moving
  climbing
  pools
  houses

Mathematics

- Favourite toys – graph. *AT1–4*
- Introduce money – *AT1, AT2*
- Comparisons of toys' prices *AT1, AT2*
- Games – counting 1–10 *AT1, AT2*
- Size comparisons *AT3*

Geography

- Playmats and routes
- Transport toys – sets of
- Making journeys – make railway/airport
- Jobs people do

Art and craft

- Draw and paint own toys or wished for toys
- Make a jigsaw
- Make a roll-along puppet
- Make a stuffed toy
- Make a peg doll
- Make hand puppet
- Catch ball game

AT1–2

English

- Discussion – favourite toys, writing descriptions
- Discussion – sorting toys into sets according to use
- Label all toys in classroom – vocabulary and initial letters
- Read stories and poems about toys
- Write own imaginative stories about toys
- Write notices and adverts for toyshop
- Make lists about different types of toys and use *AT1–3*

Religious Education

- Presents – discussion sharing and greed: discussion and read stories
- Pets as living things, *not* toys
- Toy sale for charity

History

- Make a toy museum
- Visit a toy museum
- Make a book about own toys from past
- Look at materials – old and new, for toys

1 Toys are things we play with.
2 They help us to learn.
3 There are many types of toys made of many different materials.

4 Some cost a great deal of money and some do not.
5 Some children have many toys and some do not.
6 Children and adults usually love toys.

STARTING POINTS ▶

● Make the home corner into a toyshop, either using toys that the children have loaned or toys from school. Invent a name together and write this on a large sign above the shop. You can make advertising posters saying, 'Bargain, sale, one only, special offer', and write price labels for the merchandise in multiples of 1p. Provide a toy till and play money.

place mat

My teddy

cut fringes

draw with crayons

● Have a teddy-bears' picnic, outdoors if the weather permits. Involve the children in the preparation of the food, making small sandwiches, cakes, sweets, drinks, and so on. The children can pack the food in baskets or trays and help to lay out the picnic. They could also make a place mat for themselves and their teddy. If any child doesn't have a teddy perhaps you could arrange a loan for the event.

● Have a toy day where the children are allowed to bring in a favourite toy and play with it with friends in school for a session. Those who want to can show their toy to the rest of the class and say why they like it.

● Investigate toys that move. Ask the children to bring in a toy that moves, or provide a selection yourself. Play with them and try to identify how the toy moves (does it crawl, run, roll, sail, fly?), and what makes it move.

● Have a Christmas toy collection. You can join in with one of the major charities or have one of your own.

ENGLISH ▶ CM1

Favourite toys

Ask the children to bring their favourite toy to school for one day. They can show it to the other children and tell them why they like it. Ask them to draw it then write the name of the toy on the picture. If they are able to, they can also write a piece about why they like the toy and when they play with it, where they got it from, and so on. Mount this work inside a shop shape and title it, 'Our favourite toy shop'.

You may use **Copymaster 1** (Cover sheet) for the children to write their piece in. It can also serve as a cover for the topic book, or for you to enlarge and write vocabulary on.

Make collections

Make collections of sets of toys such as dolls, boats, planes, cars, bathtime toys, sand toys, construction games, and so on. Ask the children to bring them in or use the school's own toys. Display them in large PE hoops as set rings, and label each set. See under Mathematics (p. 5) for further work on sets. You can

have a competition to see who can find the points of similarity and difference.

corrugated card roof

Our favourite toy shop

Wonderful toys

Concept marketing of toys is now very popular, whereby manufacturers produce not only the toy but a whole range of goods and play accessories to go with it, e.g. bags, lunch boxes, bedding, T-shirts, books, and so on. Make a collection of these things for the latest craze-toy popular with your children.

Labels

Gather together all the toys in the classroom and write labels for them in bold, coloured print then, with the children's help, match the labels to the toys. This may be used as an opportunity to identify initial sounds. Keep the labels in permanent use and draw the children's attention to them regularly. You may need to put small drawings on the labels if the boxes have no decoration on them indicating contents.

Read stories and poems

There are many stories and poems about toys. You can search with the children for likely books in the school or local library. Read them all and discuss with the children which they liked best and why. Did they like the characters, the action or the setting? Ask them to decide on their favourite book, then take a class vote and record the result either in the form of a graph or by displaying the favourite book.

Our favourite book

The teddy-bear's long journey

card support

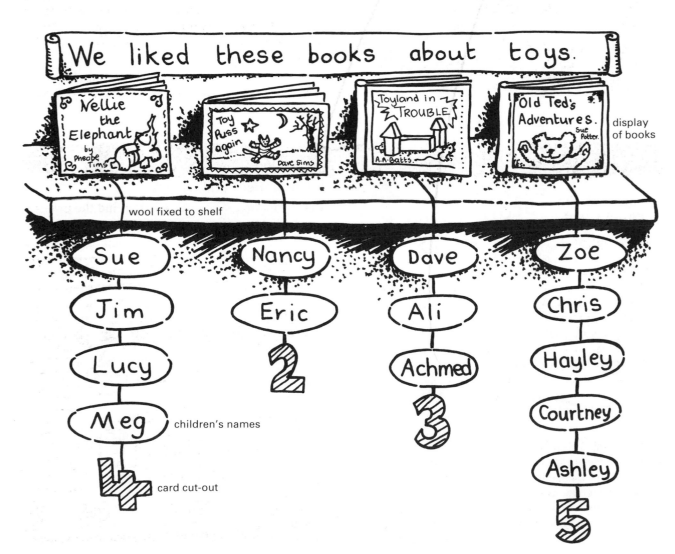

We liked these books about toys.

Nellie the Elephant by Pheobe Tims

Toy Puss again Dave Sims

Toyland in TROUBLE A.A.Batts.

Old Ted's Adventures. Sue Potter.

display of books

wool fixed to shelf

Sue
Jim
Lucy
Meg
children's names
card cut-out

Nancy
Eric
2

Dave
Ali
Achmed
3

Zoe
Chris
Hayley
Courtney
Ashley
5

Popular stories include: *Teddy-bear Robinson* by Joan G. Robinson (Puffin); *The night the toys had a party* (Enid Blyton); *Winnie the Pooh* (A.A. Milne); *Holly and Ivy* by Rummer Godden (Puffin); *This little Puffin,* published by Puffin, is an excellent anthology of poems, nursery rhymes and verses of all kinds, and has many featuring toys.

Write stories

Write a story about toys. For example: The night my toys came to life; Naughty toys; The bad toy bus; The best teddy in the world; The dolls' holiday; If I could buy any toy in the world; The runaway toy train; The bath ducks have a party.

Pick one story theme for the youngest children and discuss it together, writing vocabulary suggestions on a large, appropriately shaped, piece of paper.

You can make small books, again in an appropriate shape, for the children to write the story on. A story of only two or three lines on ordinary paper can be stretched out over four or five pages in a little book. Of course, many children may still be at the stage of under-writing and will need to dictate their story to an adult, but the book will provide a sense of achievement and further motivation. The children may want to suggest their own story titles, and you can encourage this and discuss likely characters and action.

Write notices and adverts

Make a toyshop as suggested and discuss with the children the kind of posters and notices they might see in the shop. You may have to visit a real shop to discover appropriate notices. The children can help to write their own notices, and you can also write some as a good example for them to read. Items could include prices and product names, or any of the following words: bargain, sale, reduced, way out, toilets, pay here, and so on. Encourage them to use best present-ation, perhaps including a drawn pattern round the edge.

Make lists

Working together as a class, with you as the scribe, make lists of any of the following: Toys needed in your toyshop; Notices needed for the shop; Favourite toys; Toys wished for; Toys babies like; Toys for grown ups (e.g. train sets, radio control vehicles, computer games); Toys for the bath; Toys for the sand-pit; Riding toys; Climbing toys; Small/large toys.

You can include the lists as part of your work in other curricular areas when appropriate.

Favourite type of toy

In conjunction with language work, discuss the different categories of toys that we use, for example: Construction toys and games; Ride-on toys (bikes, cars, horses, scooters, skateboards, skates); Play-inside toys (tents, houses); Climbing toys (frames, swings, slides); Table games (all boxed games, jigsaws, dice games); Small outdoor games (skipping ropes, balls); Pretend toys (dolls, soft toys, castles, tea-sets). Try to get the children to identify the sets of toys according to use and make a graph to show the favourite type of toy in the class.

Use **Copymaster 2** (Things we play with) for the children to choose from. These can then be coloured and assembled as a graph with appropriate axes.

Introduce money

Have a till and some play money in the toyshop and make some simple shopping cards which relate to the toys for sale there. The earliest cards need only be simple purchasing orders such as, 'Buy a doll for 5p'.

The shopper has to read the card and ask for the toy, then produce the correct money from a purse. Use only 1p coins at first, then slowly introduce the idea of equivalence by using 2p coins then 5p coins. Extend this with shopping cards asking for two toys. Show the coins on the cards in sets to help the addition process.

The cost of toys

Bring in toy catalogues and look through these with the children and discuss the various merits of the toys. You can help them to read the prices and tell them which are more expensive than others. They will enjoy discussing which are 'worth' more money. You can involve them in the pricing of the toys in the class shop but, at this level, the prices will all need to be in multiples of 1p, e.g. 10p, 11p, 12p, and not 10p, 15p, 20p.

Games

Make some simple counting games to sell in the shop. They can be put in decorated envelopes with a die and counters. The games should also be priced, of course.

Use **Copymaster 3** (Our game) as the blank for these games. It is a simple counting-on to ten game, with a start and finish point marked. The children can decorate it as they choose, and write on a couple of forfeits and bonuses such as, 'Go on one' or 'Go back one'.

Snakes and ladders is a useful counting game but numbers up to 100 are sometimes confusing for the early player. **Copymaster 4** (Snakes and ladders) has numbers up to 20 and can be coloured in and used by the children.

You can also produce your own snap and dominoes cards. For dominoes, cut the cards to size and mark in the centre line of the dominoes. Show the children how to draw in the dots in the recognised formations. For snap, you will need to decide on four or five different simple pictures to use and you will need about 20 or 30 cards for a good game. Get the same child to do one image on all the cards, using the same colours, so that they are as alike as possible. You can use the pictures from **Copymaster 2** (Things we play with) to make the cards.

Size

Using the toys you have collected from the children, compare them and try to order them according to properties such as size, weight and length. Make some order and vocabulary labels and display your findings for a couple of days.

Investigate toys that move

Make a collection of toys that move, and play with them to find out what makes them move and what powers them. If the toy can be dismantled easily, and has a hidden power source such as a spring or a battery, try to open it up and have a look. Sort the toys you have into sets of like-power sources and label them accordingly, e.g., 'These toys are all powered by springs'. Other power sources might be electricity, hand, wind, elastic.

Use **Copymaster 5** (Moving toys) to record your findings. You can draw more horizontal lines on the first copy if you need them, then make further copies from that one.

Investigate materials

Look carefully at the collection of different toys and help the children to identify the materials they are made from. Put them into sets according to material. You will need to have some intersecting sets as some toys use two or more materials.

Fast cars

Although it is too early at this level to construct fair tests, you can introduce the children to the idea of testing and to the fact that variables always occur which affect the outcome of the test.

Make a collection of small metal cars. Introduce hypothesis by asking the children to say which one they think will be the fastest in a race. If you ask them to give a reason for their choice, it will probably be something like, 'Because that's mine', or 'Because it's Batman's and his is fast'. So, encourage them to look at how the car is made. Will its wheels move round easily? Are they wide, narrow, large or small, and should this affect the speed of the car?

Involve them in setting up the race. Where do they think the best place is and why? Try out various surfaces such as carpet, outside path, hall floor, and discuss what happened when the cars were run on these surfaces. How did the children get the toys to move? Did one child have a stronger push than another? The main purpose of the exercise is to encourage the children to form and express ideas, to question and try to think of possible reasons for things they see.

More racing

There are many moving toys that could be used for races. For example, there are plastic frogs which leap like tiddlywinks. There are wind up creatures which twist and turn as they move forward. There are many water creatures with spring-powered fins and paddles, and these make for exciting racing in water-trays. Use this opportunity to discuss possibilities and outcomes as you did for the racing cars.

TECHNOLOGY

Design and make a wooden toy plane

The design brief is to make a toy plane in wood that is easy to handle and strong enough to be played with. Provide an assortment of wood scraps that can easily be cut, and a variety of nails, screws, bolts and glue that could be used to join the wood. You will also need a vice, preferably on a bench to make cutting easier. Use 'real' tools and teach the children how to handle the tools safely from the very beginning.

After looking at the materials available, discuss how the toy plane might be made, then ask the children to draw up a plan. The plane doesn't have to fly, but must be good to handle and look exciting. Let the children make up their design then evaluate its success.

Design a doll's-house

Discuss what play features the children would like to have in a doll's-house. This can be planned and worked on as a class project so that everyone can have an input, and it can form part of your play equipment when completed. Supply a collection of different materials which they can choose from at the planning stage. The base of the house could be the inside of a cupboard, a large plastic container, or a collection of small boxes joined together. Whatever the form, the eventual size will be dictated by the materials you use and the space you have available for its use and storage.

During the design stage, guide the children into considering the following points: the access point for play (front, back, sides or top); position of windows and doors; type of window and door (cut to open or simply drawn on); decoration.

Furnishing can be considered as a separate project.

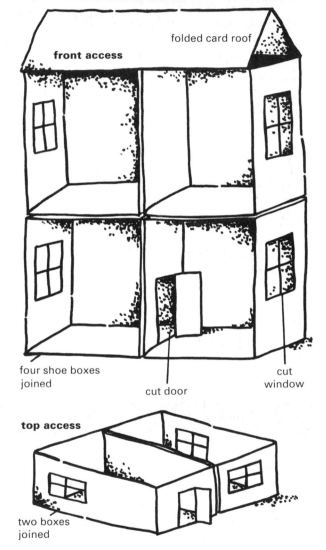

folded card roof
front access

four shoe boxes joined
cut door
cut window

top access

two boxes joined

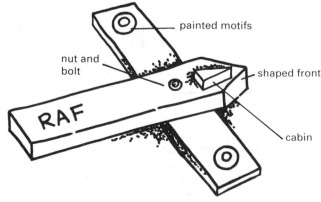

painted motifs
nut and bolt
shaped front
cabin
RAF

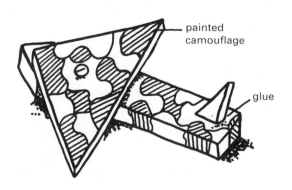

painted camouflage
glue

Construction toys

There are many types on the market now and you may already have some of the main ones in school, such as Lego©, Meccano®, Duplo®. Many of these sets can be used to teach basic mechanical and constructional principles, and as part of this topic you can either do this or give them simple design briefs such as: make a tall, very stable tower; make a house; make a bridge; make a vehicle with wheels.

It is just as viable to let the children experiment on their own during a 'construction afternoon' and see how many different things they can make from the assortment of equipment.

Designs for other people

Discuss then draw up a design for any of the following projects: a toy for a new baby; a toy for a crawling baby; a toy for a boy/girl; a toy for a grown-up.

ART AND CRAFT

Draw and paint

The subject can be favourite toys which are owned by the artist. Provide a range of different drawing and painting media and different types of paper. If possible, let the children draw from life on the day when they bring in the toy for another part of the topic. If the children can look at the thing they are drawing, they can be taught to observe details and make constant reference as they draw.

Make a jigsaw

Let the children draw a bold, simple picture with felt tips on white card. The artist can then cut it into six pieces to make the jigsaw. Provide an envelope for storing the pieces and draw the same picture on the front for reference.

A roll-along puppet

Provide a 15 cm long piece of white card for the children to draw a figure on. It can be of any subject but must be drawn without legs. The legs are drawn on an 8 cm circle of card as illustrated, then fixed to the back of the figure with a paper-fastener so that it turns

freely. A length of card can be fixed with Sellotape® to the back of the figure for the push-along handle. You will need to experiment with different surfaces for the figure to run on, and this itself should stimulate an investigation. The figure can be decorated with glitter, sequins and other small items.

Make a stuffed toy

Cut out very simple shapes from felt, as shown, with little emphasis on limbs and narrow shapes. The cutting of fabric is too difficult for most children at this level, but the following processes are suitable with adult supervision.

Each toy will need two matching sides which can be stuck together with Copydex Adhesive – an excellent glue for fabric. Use only a little round the edge, leaving a space for stuffing, and then leave overnight to dry. Decorate with scraps of felt, wool, ribbon, sequins, and so on, then stuff lightly with kapok or other material, sealing the hole with Copydex on the inside edges. A ribbon loop can be glued to the top to make a baby toy or a hanger for a car. Those who don't want to make a doll or a teddy can make a 'Turtle', with its coloured

paper-fastener

handle

glue

push along

centre

legs opposite each other

circle rolls to make legs move round

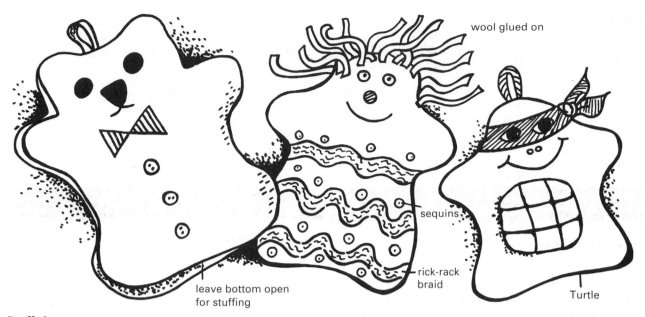

Stuffed toy

bandana made from felt and glued into position. Felt tips can be used to decorate the eyes and mouth.

A peg doll

Let the children select their own fabric, then cut it out for them using pinking-shears to deter fraying. Use felt tips for the children to draw a face on the top of the peg. Next help them to do a row of running stitches at the top end of the fabric, using a strong thread. This is then gathered round the neck of the peg and the threads secured by wrapping them round and tying at the back. Spread the skirt round evenly.

Cut about ten long strands of wool for hair, and put

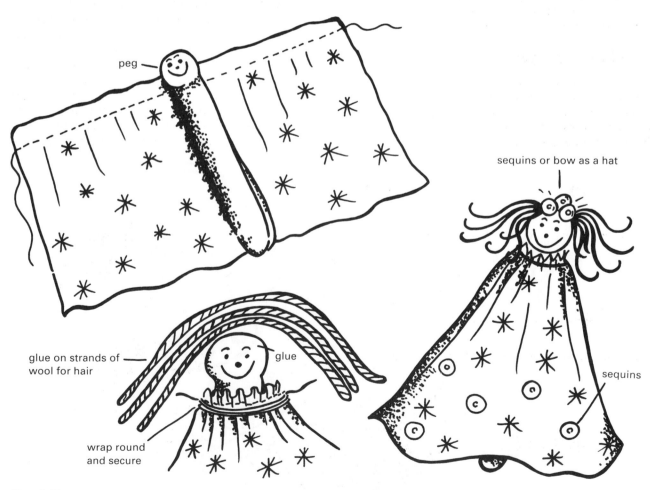

Peg doll

a blob of Copydex Adhesive on the top of the head to which you should press the wool as shown. Hold in place for a short while until fixed. The top of the head can be decorated with sequins or a bow of ribbon.

Puppets

See the topic on 'My body' for some ideas for puppets.

Catch ball

Decorate a plastic yogurt pot with a mixture of PVA glue and paint (this sticks to plastic) then stick on a 30 cm length of wool to the edge, using Sellotape®, as shown. Make a tight ball of tissue-paper secured with Sellotape®, or use a ready-made tissue ball and fix this

to the other end of the wool. Now it is ready to play with. The object of the game is to hold the pot, swing the ball up and then catch it in the pot.

MUSIC

Listen to the *Nutcracker*

Listen to, or if possible go and see, the *Nutcracker* by Tchaikovsky, then discuss with the children what they think about the composer's interpretation of the toys and other subjects. You may also need to read the story.

Sing songs

Sing nursery songs such as the 'Teddy-bears' picnic', 'Miss Polly had a dolly', 'I know a teddy-bear'. You can use toys to help the singing along. For example, if you can find a few toy frogs you could use them to help illustrate counting songs such as, 'Five little speckled frogs', or with plastic bath ducks sing, 'Five little ducks went swimming one day'. The nursery anthology published by Puffin, *This little Puffin*, has a collection of rhymes about toys and related subjects. See also

Counting songs, produced by the Early Learning Centre.

Play instruments

Use a variety of non-tuned percussion instruments and experiment with the sounds they make with toys in mind. Talk about which sounds seem to be like a toy. For example, does a deep, slow drumbeat sound like a teddy-bear? Does a rickrack put them in mind of a fast car? Do the bells sound like a fairy doll?

Make instruments

Toyshops often sell musical instruments, and the children would enjoy making their own simple ones to play with. Use some of the ideas shown here.

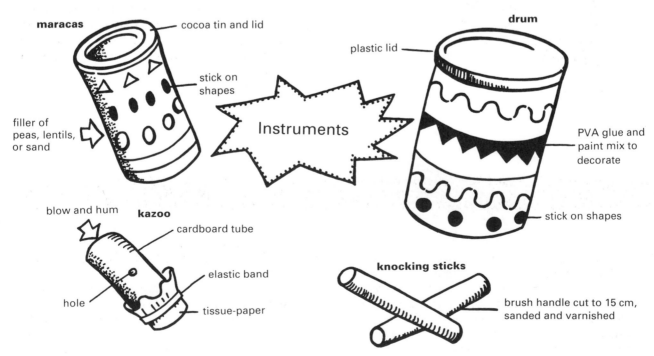

Instruments

10

DANCE

Toys and music

Listen to the *Nutcracker* and discuss which parts the children think sound like which toys. Ask them to move like a rag doll, a teddy-bear, a toy robot, a fast car, a plane, a Scalextric® car, a ball, a skipping rope. Discuss what movements each might make then try them out to whichever part of the *Nutcracker* sounds appropriate. For example, the 'Russian Dance', with its speed, energy and trills, could be good for fast cars.

DRAMA

A teddy-bears' picnic

As mentioned under Starting Points (p. 2), let the children bring in their own teddies, or make teddy masks so that the children themselves can be the bears.

card circlet

back view

staples

position of card circlet

The mask illustrated below fits on the head like a sun visor, so that the child still has clear vision. Discuss with the children what sort of games the bears might like to play and how they would behave at a picnic so that they can get into the role.

In the same way you could have a dolls' tea party.

Make a toyshop

With drama as the starting point this time, talk about what sort of people we find in shops, how they behave, and what sort of things they say. You can initiate some imaginary situations in a casual way as the children play in the shop. Ask one to be a naughty child, another a mother, and one the shopkeeper, then let them improvise from there. At other times, do this sort of thing with the rest of the class or a group as an audience and let everyone give suggestions or join in with the action.

PE

Play with large toys

As part of your toy day, let the children bring in a riding toy or borrow one from the nursery, if you have one attached to your school. Make sure everyone has a go, and ask observers and riders to see which parts of the body are being used to move the toy. You could have short races on grass or in the playground to see which surface is easiest to move on. Construct a figure-of-eight track for movement trials.

Using large climbing frames, folding tunnels and other climbing toys, let the children explore their movements, pulling themselves along, upwards or round the obstacles, thinking about what parts of the body they are using each time.

If weather permits you may feel like trying out a paddling pool in the same sort of way!

RELIGIOUS EDUCATION ▶

Presents

Discuss the idea of presents, talking with the children about things they have received, things they have given to whom, and the different occasions for giving and receiving presents. If it is appropriate, you can discuss what it might be like to receive no presents at all. Although this will be fairly abstract for the children, it is good to introduce them to the idea. You can also talk about what constitutes a present. Is it something bought or made by the giver? Can it be a handwritten card, such as the children make at school, or a letter, or something like a kiss?

Use **Copymaster 6** (A Christmas stocking), which is an outline of a Christmas stocking, for the children to draw or write either a list or a piece about any of the following: Presents I have given to Mum or Dad; Presents I would like; Presents I would give to poor children (here or abroad); Presents for the garden birds.

Moral matters

Talk about sharing and greed or selfishness. These matters usually come up fairly regularly in the course of an infant day. The children will have plenty of opportunity to share in a more personally significant situation if you have a share a toy day, when they can each bring in a favourite toy from home for the day.

To help along discussion and build up the body of understanding, read any of the following, which put the concepts in a story context: *Cinderella*; *Pinocchio*; 'The three wishes'; *Snow White and the seven dwarves*; *Teddy-bear Robinson* by Joan G. Robinson (Puffin); *My naughty little sister* by Dorothy Edwards (Puffin); *Tyrone the dirty rotten cheat* by Hans Wilhelm (Hippo); and many Enid Blyton stories including *The night the toys had a party* which is about sharing.

Pets

Some children and adults confuse pets with toys and this topic is a good opportunity to highlight the differences. Contact National Canine Defence League, who produce the nationally famous logo, 'A dog is for life, not just Christmas', and they will be able to supply posters and information about pets as live creatures. Try to bring in a pet (firstly check with DES regulations about pets in schools) and compare it with a toy, trying to find as many similarities and differences as possible between a live animal and a non-living article. Let the children handle both and talk about the daily needs of the live creature.

A toy sale

Car boot sales are popular, and the children may be familiar with the idea of 'bring and buy'. Have a collection of good unwanted toys and comics, and have a toy sale in aid of a charity. The children can help with the pricing and selling, which can be in class or within the school.

HISTORY

Toy museums

If there is a toy museum in your area, it can prove an inspiring but sometimes frustrating trip, as the toys often can't be played with. However, you can make your own toy museum with a hands-on facility. Ask the children to bring toys to school which they used to play with in the recent past. These can be displayed with the name and age of the owner when the toys were played with, and the name of the toy. The toys can then be collected in a museum corner with a play area attached if the owners agree.

If possible, collect some toys from the parents' childhood too, and display these with a photograph of the owner and a label with the name of the toy and the parent.

Use **Copymaster 7** (Past and present) for the children to record some details of toys used in the past by themselves or their parents. The details can be drawn pictures, cut-out pictures, or words. You can enlarge the sheet to write vocabulary on.

The children's own baby toys displayed with a photograph of the owner are always interesting and provoke much discussion about, 'when we were only babies – last year!'.

Make a book

To introduce the children to historical documentation, make a zig-zag book about their baby toys or current favourites. The children can put their name and the date on the front, and draw a different toy on each page. Show them to the children later in the year so that they can see a record from their immediate past.

Look at materials

Help the children to identify the materials that new and old toys are made from. Toys from parents' childhood may be metal, plastic and fabrics; or for older parents and grandparents they may be ceramic, wood, metal and various fabrics. Modern toys rely heavily on the use of plastics and metals. Take a couple of toys and label all the materials used, for example plastic eyes on a fur fabric or sheepskin teddy-bear, and metals, plastics and the chemicals in the batteries of a toy car.

GEOGRAPHY ▶

Playmats and routes

Playmats which portray roads in town and countryside are useful to help the children towards following a route. Use small cars and other vehicles and small boxes for buildings. Introduce the idea of following a route by talking as you play, 'Take your car straight across the traffic lights to the garage, John', 'Turn left to the hospital, Susan', and so on.

Let the children draw out their own playmat, putting in their own landscape features such as a river and a bridge, a field, a park or the local swimming pool. Use pencil to do the rough, then colour over with felt tips on heavy quality paper. Alternatively, you could use strips of paper for them to stick down and build up into a road system, adding drawn buildings, such as their own houses.

Transport

Collect as many different forms of transport toys as possible, then sort them into sets of cars, lorries, planes, trains, construction and service vehicles such as the emergency services. Talk about the different uses of the vehicles and set up play situations in the sand-pit, in a patch of soil outside, in the water-tray, or on the road mat. You could have a quarry near the sea, or a building site in the middle of a town. The children can play at quarrying and shifting the materials to a building site. They may want to play through an experience of their own such as a car crash, or they may

want to act out a situation they have seen in a story or on television. For example, 'Thunderbirds 4' may be needed for an underwater rescue of a submarine crew trapped in your water-tray.

Making journeys

Still using the toy vehicles, talk about the different ways to make a journey and sort out the vehicles needed in different situations. You could set up a railway station with all the attendant vehicles. Duplo® and Lego® have rails and the blocks for building construction. Airports and ports can also be made, and a trip to the school library to find a book about airports or planes could provide useful information to extend the play as the children see how the area is layed out, and what the different vehicles do. This sort of reference, and conversation with an adult as they play, can enhance the value of the learning situation.

Jobs people do

Many toys relate to the different jobs people do. We can buy doctor, nurse and firefighter outfits, and others can be made easily, sometimes just with a hat. A policeman can be created from a notepad, a toy radio set and a flat, dark blue hat, available from parental job sources. Set up role-play situations in conjunction with the toy shop, for example: a policeman could come to talk about security; a telephone engineer could install a new phone; someone could fall ill and an ambulance could be called; there could be a fire; new toys could be delivered; a salesperson could bring a toy catalogue for an order; the postman could call with letters.

Small toys, such as Duplo®, Lego® and Playmobil®, have the emergency services toy vehicles and the relevant people. They also produce ordinary people and buildings which can be made into shops, offices, houses, and so on. There are farm set-ups, harbours and other work situations, but the children can always make buildings from cardboard boxes or construction bricks, and change ordinary cars into something else with self-adhesive stickers.

Toys 1

Things we play with

play inside

small outdoor

climbing

pretend

table games

construction

riding

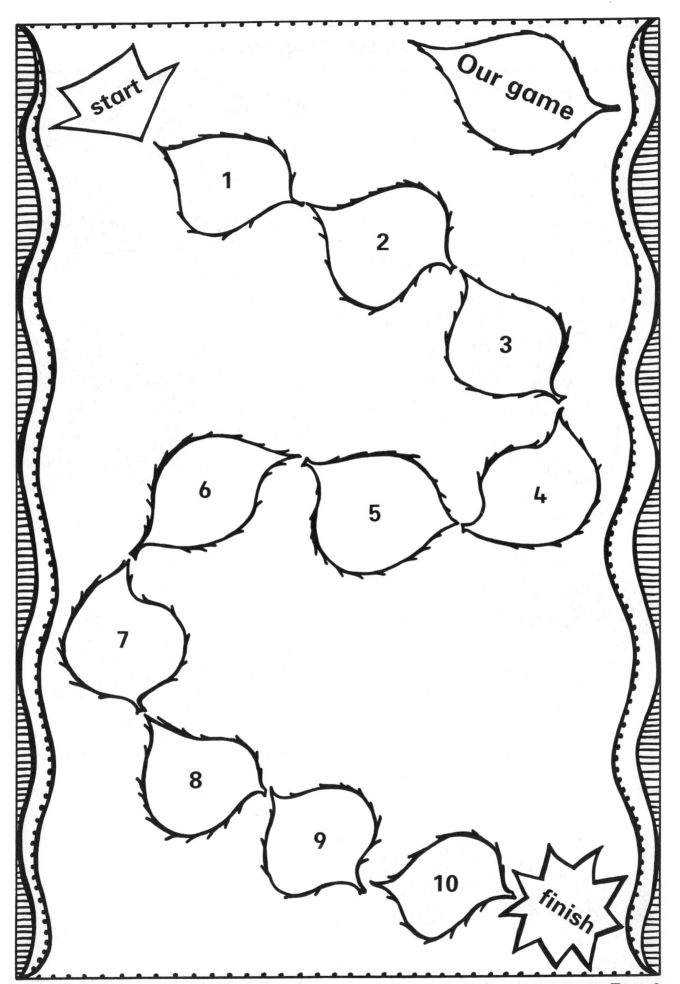

start

Our game

1

2

3

6

5

4

7

8

9

10

finish

Toys 3

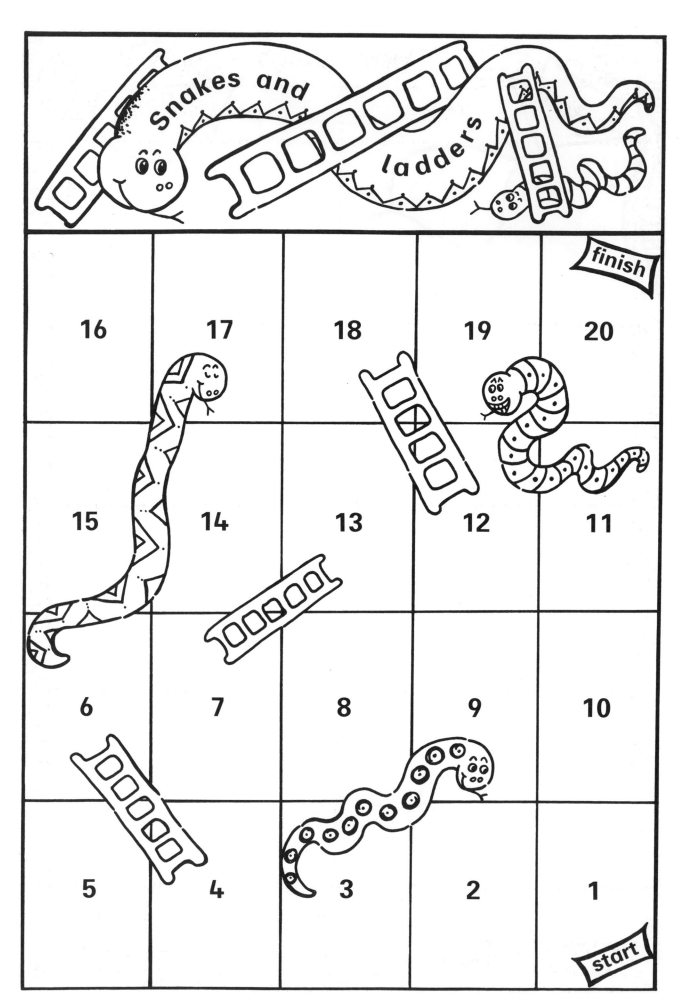

Toys 4

Moving toys

Toy	moved by

spring	electricity	hand	wind	elastic

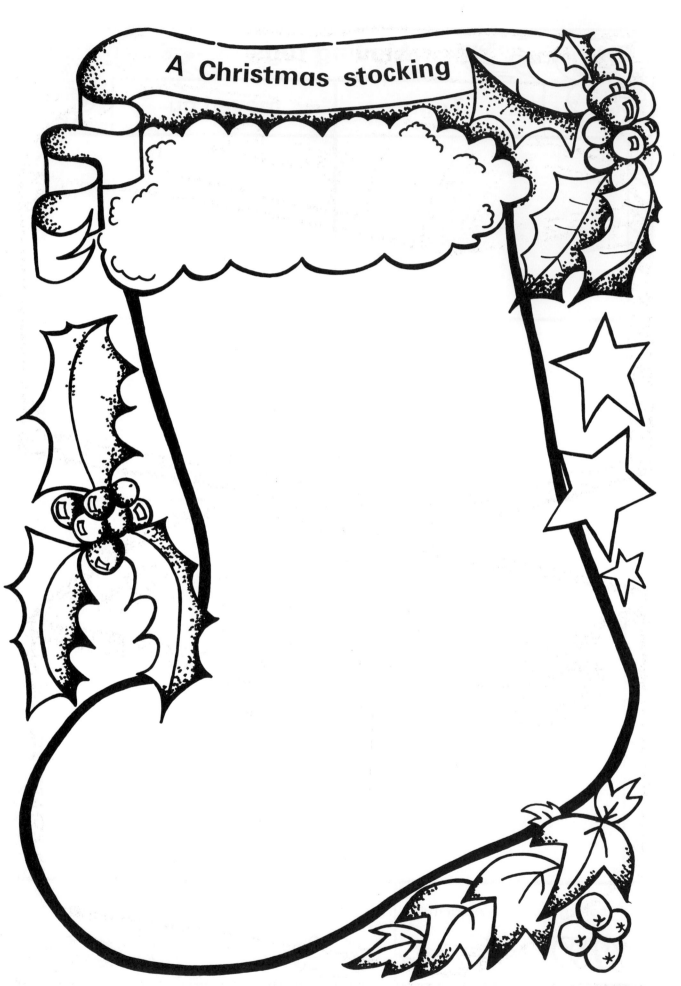

A Christmas stocking

Toys 6

Past and present

past

present

AIR

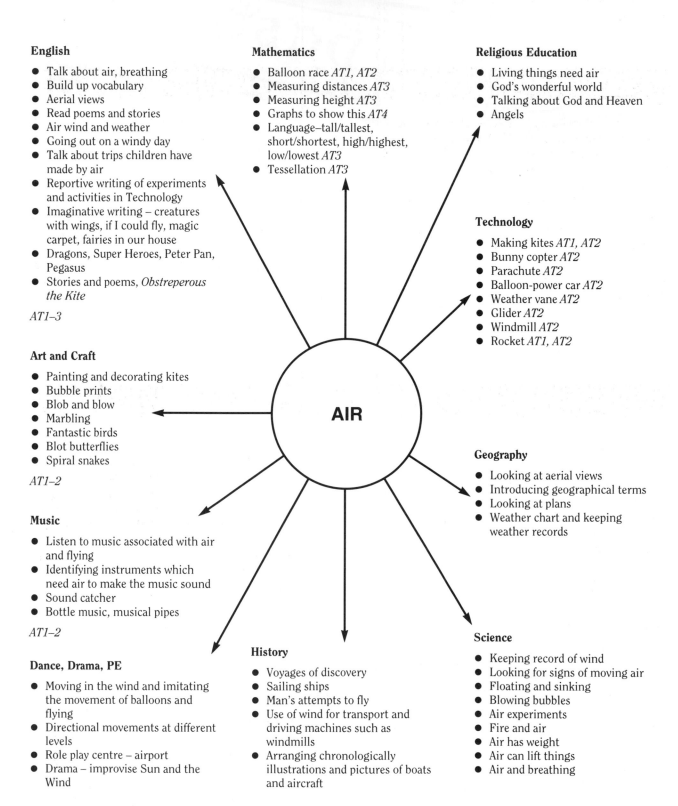

English

- Talk about air, breathing
- Build up vocabulary
- Aerial views
- Read poems and stories
- Air wind and weather
- Going out on a windy day
- Talk about trips children have made by air
- Reportive writing of experiments and activities in Technology
- Imaginative writing – creatures with wings, if I could fly, magic carpet, fairies in our house
- Dragons, Super Heroes, Peter Pan, Pegasus
- Stories and poems, *Obstreperous the Kite*

AT1–3

Art and Craft

- Painting and decorating kites
- Bubble prints
- Blob and blow
- Marbling
- Fantastic birds
- Blot butterflies
- Spiral snakes

AT1–2

Music

- Listen to music associated with air and flying
- Identifying instruments which need air to make the music sound
- Sound catcher
- Bottle music, musical pipes

AT1–2

Dance, Drama, PE

- Moving in the wind and imitating the movement of balloons and flying
- Directional movements at different levels
- Role play centre – airport
- Drama – improvise Sun and the Wind

Mathematics

- Balloon race *AT1, AT2*
- Measuring distances *AT3*
- Measuring height *AT3*
- Graphs to show this *AT4*
- Language–tall/tallest, short/shortest, high/highest, low/lowest *AT3*
- Tessellation *AT3*

History

- Voyages of discovery
- Sailing ships
- Man's attempts to fly
- Use of wind for transport and driving machines such as windmills
- Arranging chronologically illustrations and pictures of boats and aircraft

Religious Education

- Living things need air
- God's wonderful world
- Talking about God and Heaven
- Angels

Technology

- Making kites *AT1, AT2*
- Bunny copter *AT2*
- Parachute *AT2*
- Balloon-power car *AT2*
- Weather vane *AT2*
- Glider *AT2*
- Windmill *AT2*
- Rocket *AT1, AT2*

Geography

- Looking at aerial views
- Introducing geographical terms
- Looking at plans
- Weather chart and keeping weather records

Science

- Keeping record of wind
- Looking for signs of moving air
- Floating and sinking
- Blowing bubbles
- Air experiments
- Fire and air
- Air has weight
- Air can lift things
- Air and breathing

BASIC CONCEPTS

1 Air is all around us.

2 We need air to live.

3 We breathe air through our lungs.

4 Wind is moving air.

5 Air is a force which can move things.

6 Wind brings weather.

7 Animals and humans can travel through air.

STARTING POINTS

● Make a collection of objects, pictures, photographs and posters connected with air. Include such things as toy aeroplanes, propellers, sail-boats, kites, musical instruments, bicycle pumps, air-bed inflators, a hair-dryer, a vacuum-cleaner, fans. Display pictures of windmills, gliders, hot-air balloons, and pictures of different types of weather and wind, from gentle breeze to storm and hurricane. Look for signs of moving air in photographs.

● Collect books of a suitable reading level which have good illustrations. Read story-books, poems and show videos, such as *Peter Pan*, *Dumbo*, *Chitty Chitty Bang Bang*, *The red balloon*. Read Greek legends, for example Pegasus, the flying horse, and a simplified story of Icarus, who flew too near the sun. Superman, and other super heroes who can fly, can be included if desired. Look at wildlife videos of birds in flight and winged insects.

● Visit transport museums to look at early flying machines and, if possible, compare them with modern aircraft by visiting an airport. The Museum of Science and Technology in Manchester has a good collection of aircraft, as does the Naval Base Museum at Yeovilton, where you can actually go on board the first Concorde. Many children will have experienced air travel when going on holiday and they can talk about their experiences.

ENGLISH

CM1

Breathing

Talk about breathing, it is something we all do without thinking about it. Sit the children down and quietly discuss the way we breathe, what happens when we breathe in, and what happens when we breathe out. Then take them to an open space where they can run around as fast as they can. Let them do this for a few minutes then ask them to sit down and talk about how they feel. Is it easy to talk? Why do they think they are having to breathe faster than before?

Look at birds flying

Watch videos of birds flying. Look at the way they swoop and glide and hover. Do all the birds fly the same way? Contrast, if possible, the golden eagle and the tiny humming bird. Why does the little bird have to flap its wings so fast, when the eagle can soar and glide high in the air? The children can try to imagine what it would feel like to be able to fly. If possible, try to get hold of a video of views taken from an aeroplane. This will help to give the children a sense of what it would be like to look down from a great height.

Windy day

Read poems and stories about air, wind and weather, flying, toy and hot-air balloons, windmills and kites.

Take the children out on a windy day and let them feel the wind as it blows their hair and themselves about. Let them fly kites and observe things being moved by the wind, such as litter, leaves, trees, washing hanging on a line, and clouds moving across the sky. All these first-hand experiences will help the children to talk and write about air and wind.

Copymaster 1 (Cover sheet) can be used as a cover for the topic folder with the title written in the middle of the sheet. Pictures connected with the topic can be cut from magazines, or the children can draw their own and stick them in the space. The sheet can also be used as a personal vocabulary list or enlarged for use as a class list, with the children suggesting what words they will need.

Reportive writing

Ask the children to write about any trips they may have made in an aeroplane, for example when going away on holiday. They could also write from their direct experience of going out on a windy day, or of any Science activities and Technology tasks they may have undertaken, such as making a windmill or a rocket. Written observations of the birds that come to a bird table the children have set up, or keeping a simple record of the weather over a period of time, would also be appropriate.

Creative writing

Use pictures of creatures with wings to stimulate the children's imagination for creative writing. Talk about the various creatures. This should cover a great variety, from birds and insects, to fairies, dragons and flying dinosaurs. The children can imagine flying with wings, or as a super hero, or by some other means such as a magic carpet, a flying cloak, or a broomstick. See *Blueprints Writing* for extra copymaster sheets on: Space journey, Fairies in our house, Magic carpet, My dragon. See also *Blueprints Topics 5–8* (p. 101) for a sheet on Pegasus the winged horse.

Reading

Read poems and verses such as, 'The balloon seller' by Elizabeth Flemming; 'The kite' by Pearl Forbes McEwen in *Book of a thousand poems* (Evans); and 'The balloon man' and 'Bubbles' in *Come follow me* (Evans). Stories to read include, *Obstreperous the kite* (Picture Puffin); *Me and my flying machines* by Mayer (Picture Lyons); *Pooh Bear and the honey* by A.A. Milne; *Postman Pat's windy day* by Roger Hargreaves; and *Matthew blows soap bubbles* by Burke.

MATHEMATICS

Balloon race

Use **Copymaster 2** (Balloon race) to play this game. The game provides practice in counting on, and in recognising numbers either up to five or up to ten. Use a spinner marked off in five or ten sections, depending upon the ability of the children. You will also need two or more counters or buttons. The game can be for two to four players, and each player must spin a five to start. Once started, if the spinner lands on number three then the counter is moved three spaces, and so on, moving the correct number of spaces to match the number the spinner lands on. If the counter lands on a wind square it has to go back two spaces. The first to reach home is the winner. An alternative race: put two sums in each box as a calculation race.

Measuring distances

Give the children ping-pong balls and jumbo straws. They can then blow the balls as far as they can from a starting point. Using non-standard units of measurement, they can then check to see whose ball has travelled the furthest, and measure it. Try this on a variety of surfaces to see if this has any effect on the way the ball moves and the distance it travels. Does the ball go in a straight line? A graph can be made to illustrate the distances travelled.

Who jumps highest?

Ask the children to stand next to the wall, reach up as high as they can and make a mark. Then ask the children to jump up as high as they can, and make another mark. Compare the marks made by all the children and try to find out what the result shows us. Ask questions such as, 'Does the tallest child also jump the highest?' This can be checked by looking at the distance between each child's two marks, and actually measuring the gap. The teacher may have to do this but it should create a lot of class discussion. The distances can be measured with lengths of wool, and

these can be laid out side by side for the children to see which is the longest. There may be some discussion about who is tallest and who jumped the highest, so it may be as well to talk about the use of language such as tall/tallest, short/shortest, high/highest, low/lowest. A class display can be made to illustrate this.

Tessellation

Tessellation can also be included here if desired, since the children will be looking at the flight of insects, and bees make shapes which tessellate when making the honeycomb.

SCICE

(SCIENCE)

Moving air

Collect together lots of pictures which illustrate wind and weather. Go outside on a windy day and let the children experience the difficulties of running against the wind, even more difficult if they hold a large piece of cardboard and try to run.

Keep a record of the wind every day, and look for signs of moving air all around us.

Look at **Copymaster 3** (Moving air) and see if there are any clues in the picture that the air is moving. The children can draw a circle around those parts of the picture which show that the air is moving.

We can tell how strong the wind is by looking at the way it moves things in the environment. A simple wind-scale is illustrated below.

The first picture shows a flag hanging straight down, and the wind is described as calm. The second picture shows washing flapping in the air, and this is described as a breeze. The third picture shows trees swaying, with leaves and bits of branch flying through the air. This is described as a gale. Finally, where trees are uprooted and there is structural damage, this is described as a storm.

Let the children make their own simple wind indicator to help them record the wind type. Take a cardboard tube and attach strips of coloured tissue to the top. The children can then go out into the centre of the playground at the same time each day, and check the indicator. The stronger the wind, the more the strips of tissue will be blown around.

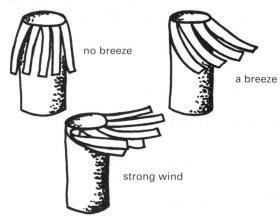

By varying the material that the strips are made of, the children could make a more accurate wind indicator. First of all, sort the strips into a simple order from the lightest to the heaviest, and place them in a row. The wind indicator can then show which of the

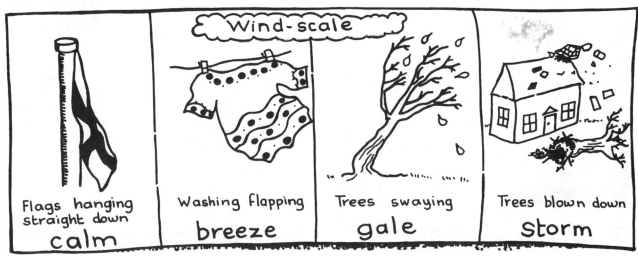

Wind-scale			
Flags hanging straight down	Washing flapping	Trees swaying	Trees blown down
calm	**breeze**	**gale**	**storm**

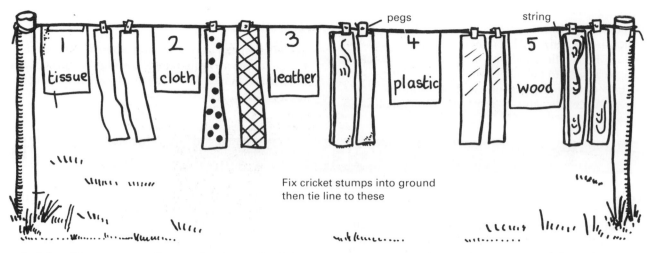

pegs   string

1 tissue
2 cloth
3 leather
4 plastic
5 wood

Fix cricket stumps into ground
then tie line to these

materials will move, according to the strength of the wind. The materials could be numbered accordingly, so that if, for example, the wind could only move the tissue, then the wind strength for that day would be one. If the wind was able to move the strips of wood, then the wind strength for that day would be five.

Floating experiments

Give the children lots of different containers and a see-through plastic bottle. Using a water trough, let them experiment to see what floats and what sinks. The children can sort and categorise the various floaters and sinkers. See *Blueprints Topics* 5–8 (p. 60), for a copymaster sheet on floating and sinking.

Look at the objects which hold air, and let the children investigate the relationship between things which hold air and things which do not. Look at the way some of the objects float. Some float on the surface of the water, while others hang just below the surface. Take a large sponge and place this on the water. Look at the way it floats. Now push it under the water and

squeeze all the air out. Does it still float in the same way? Try to get the children to explain this.

Place the plastic bottle on the water and observe how it floats. Then push it below the surface, letting the children see the air bubbles as the air escapes. Give them a plastic tube and ask them to try and re-float the bottle. They may need your help in solving this problem.

Blowing bubbles

Mix some water and washing-up liquid with a few drops of glycerine. You can make giant bubbles with a

26

wire coat-hanger, and while the bubbles are hanging in the air, encourage the children to look at the swirling colours on the surface. This can also be a good starting point for imaginative writing.

Try to get hold of different wire shapes to look at the way bubbles form. The film always covers the smallest surface area. The children can try to guess what shape the bubble will be as each of the different shapes is dipped into the mixture.

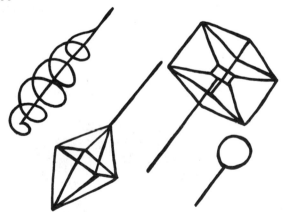

Simple air experiments

These simple experiments should be done by an adult working with a small group of children.

Fire and air

Place a candle on a dish and hold it in place with a piece of Plasticine® to stop it falling over. The adult lights the candle and the children watch it burn. Then the adult places the jar over the top of the candle. Before doing this, ask the children what they think will happen. When the jar is in position, the flame flickers and after a few seconds it goes out. Ask the children why this happened.

The flame goes out because it has used up all the oxygen in the jar, and the flame cannot burn without oxygen.

Air has weight

Air seems to have no weight, but it does. Take a long wooden bar and find its centre, then tie a piece of thread around the wood at this point. Tape one balloon to each end of the bar. The bar will balance because the balloons have the same weight. Take one balloon off the bar and blow it up. Ask the children if they think the balloon will still balance when you put the blown-up balloon back on the bar. The bar will tip down at the inflated balloon end, because the air inside it has made it heavier than the empty one.

Air can lift things

Give the children a balloon and ask them if they can think of a way that the balloon might lift a small pile of books. Give them time to investigate and try out their ideas. If no one can think of the solution, put the balloon underneath the pile of books with the end sticking out over the edge of the table. Blow into the balloon and, as it inflates, the books will be raised.

All living things need air

Talk about the earth in space, using large colour photographs to show the layer of atmosphere all around earth, and the layer of clouds too. Talk about all living things needing air, and go on to talk about our own bodies. Our lungs inside our chest are just like two balloons. They fill with air as we breathe in, and make our chest expand. Oxygen from the air goes into our blood. As we breathe out, so the air escapes and our lungs deflate. Ask the children to say how long they can hold their breath. Use a timer and they will be surprised at how short a time will actually have passed before they need to take a deep breath.

Wind power

Discuss wind power and the sails of a boat and a windmill. A good activity is to make a boat from wood off-cuts or empty butter tubs. Then design different sails and test them to see which is best at making the boat go.

TECHNOLOGY

CM4

Make kites

Make kites in the usual design with two garden canes in the form of a cross with a diamond shaped body, or take a plastic bag and attach the string to the two corners as shown.

Make sure the bag is reinforced at the two points where the string is attached, then the kite can be flown in the usual way. Warn the children of the dangers of flying kites near overhead power lines.

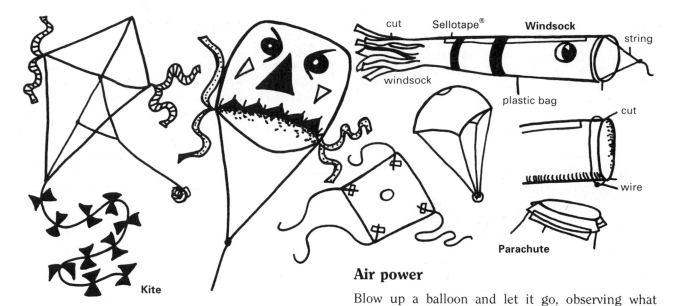

Windsock

cut   Sellotape®
windsock
plastic bag
string
cut
wire

Parachute

Kite

Bunnycopter

Use **Copymaster 4** (Bunnycopter) to colour in, and cut around the shape to stick on a piece of card. Then cut out carefully around the lines of the bunnycopter. Bend one ear forward and the other back. Let it fall from a suitable height and the bunnycopter will spin down to the ground. Use paper clips as weights on the neck to give impetus to flight. Experiment with the number you need.

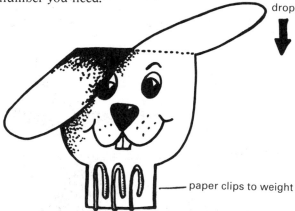

drop

paper clips to weight

Paper experiment

Take two sheets of paper from the same pile, and screw one sheet up into a ball. Hold both pieces at the same height and ask the children which one they think will land first. Air pushes up on the pieces as they drop, the flat sheet is a bigger shape so more air can push against it. This makes it fall more slowly than the ball.

Make a parachute

Take a piece of paper or light material about 30 cm square, and cut a small hole in the centre. Take four pieces of strong cotton thread, all the same length, and fix one piece to each corner.

Attach a piece of Plasticine® to the other end of the threads and test the parachute by dropping it from as high a height as possible. Make sure the children do not climb on to ladders or chairs without adult super-vision. Try to find out what will happen if we cut more holes in the parachute.

Air power

Blow up a balloon and let it go, observing what happens. Why does it do this?

Make a balloon-power car

The children can make a chassis from one of the construction kits in school, or use one of their own larger free-running cars or trucks. Alternatively, they can construct their own frame by taking two strips of wood, one long and one short, and making a cross shape. They should then fix one wheel on to either end of the short piece, and place a third wheel at the side of the end of the longer piece. This is illustrated in the diagram below.

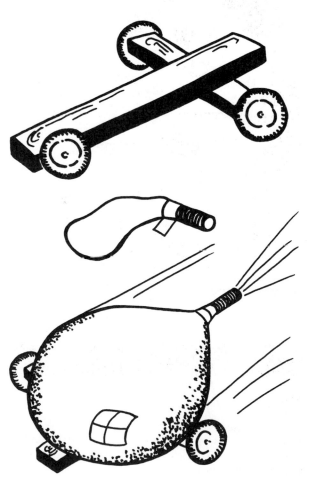

Cut off the end of a balloon and stretch it tightly over the end of a piece of plastic tubing. The tubing should be just slightly bigger than the neck of the balloon. Affix the balloon securely to the tube with sticky tape.

Attach the balloon and the tube to the vehicle with more sticky tape, and inflate the balloon by blowing through the tubing. Put your finger over the end of the tube to stop the air coming out, then place the vehicle on the floor. When you are ready, let the air come out. The car should move quickly. If it does not, check the smooth running of the wheels and the surface over which it is to travel. Give the children an opportunity to design, make and test their own machines.

Weather-vane

Take a piece of card and mark on it the directions north, south, east and west. Early in the morning, go outside and place the card so that east points towards the sun. This will ensure that the directions are in the right place. Cut out a large arrow from cardboard, and tape it to a cotton-reel. Glue a circle of card on the top.

Make the tail of the arrow very wide so that it will catch the wind. Put a blob of Plasticine® in the middle of the directions board, and stick in a plastic knitting needle, point upwards. Now place the cotton-reel on top and check that it balances and swings quite easily. Place some flat stones or pebbles on the corners of the directions board to keep it flat. The arrow will swing and point in the direction the wind is coming from.

The children can then keep a record of the direction of the wind, as well as the strength of it, by making a simple chart.

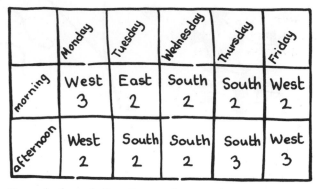

	Monday	Tuesday	Wednesday	Thursday	Friday
morning	West 3	East 2	South 2	South 2	West 2
afternoon	West 2	South 2	South 2	South 3	West 3

Record of wind direction and strength

Make a glider

The children will need help to make this, and to ensure good straight folds and creases. Follow the instructions in four simple steps:

1 Fold a sheet of stiff paper lengthways, then open the paper and fold two of the corners inward as shown.

2 Fold the new corners marked * down to the middle.

3 The corners will meet in the middle. Then fold both sides of the plane together with the folded corners inside.

4 Fold the top edges down, one at a time, to make a wing on each side.

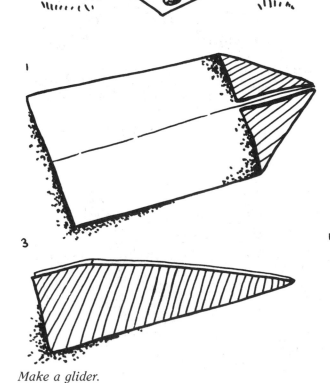

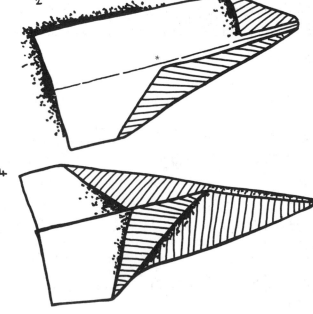

Make a glider.

Let the children test to see whose glider goes farthest. After they have made this one, let them experiment and try to improve on the design.

Make a windmill

Take a square of paper and paint or colour a design on both sides. Cut from the corners towards the centre but do not go all the way. Mark corners as shown, and then take each of the marked corners to the centre, pushing a pin through all the points at the centre to make the sails.

Now put a small bead on the end of the pin at the back of the sails, and fix the whole thing to a stick to complete the windmill.

Make a rocket

You will need a thin straw and a jumbo straw. Make sure that the thin straw fits easily into the big one. Make a cone shape and cut the end of it off, then push the thick straw through the hole in the cone. Fasten the thick straw to the cone and make sure the end of the big straw is sealed. Insert the thin straw into the wide straw and blow. We have lift off!

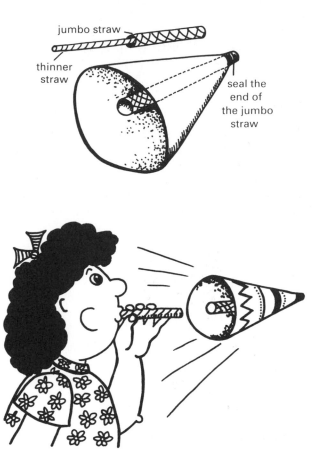

Make a windmill.

Make a rocket.

ART AND CRAFT

Painting and decorating kites

When you have made the kite, think of different ways of decorating it. You can have patterns of dots or stripes, or different coloured quarters. Grotesque faces or printed patterns made from cotton-reels, ends of boxes and cardboard tubes, are possible ideas.

Decorate kites.

Bubble prints

Mix paint, water and washing-up liquid, and put some of each colour into separate plastic tubs. Use a straw to blow bubbles until they rise above the level of the rim of the tub. You can then print from this by placing a piece of paper over the top of the tub. By repeating this several times with different colours, you can create interesting patterns.

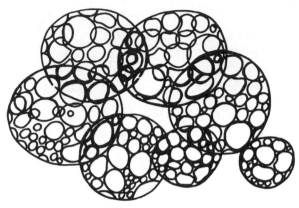

Bubble prints

Blob and blow

Drop a blob of watery paint on to a sheet of paper, and blow it around using a straw. The blown paint leaves a spidery track on the paper. You can use different coloured blobs of paint on the same sheet, or, alternatively, use black or white paint on a range of coloured papers.

Marbling

Use a shallow tray or baking tin with a rim of at least 2.5 cm (1 inch) depth, and large enough to hold the size of paper you wish to marble. Fill the tin almost to the top with water, and add a few drops of vinegar. Drop small amounts of oil-based paint on to the surface of the water, and swirl them around with a stick, pencil, or cardboard comb. Place the paper gently on the surface of the water, making sure there are no air bubbles. Gently lift the paper off and lay it coloured side up on some newspaper to dry. Once dry, the marbled paper can be displayed as a flat piece of artwork, or it can be used to make interesting display of multi-coloured fans.

Fantastic birds

Cut out bird shapes, and attach strips and curls, and hand shapes of different coloured paper as beautiful feathers. These can then be hung from the ceiling as mobiles.

Blot butterflies

Dab blots of paint on the inside crease of a sheet of folded paper. Fold the paper again, and press the paint into fantastic shapes. When the sheet is opened out it will reveal a shape that looks like the wings of a butterfly. Paint in the body and antennae, then cut out and display. This technique can also be used to make the bodies of the insects, and with the addition of large cellophane® wings stuck to the back, they can hang as fantastic insects.

string or
crepe
paper

Blot butterflies

32

Spiral snakes
Opening cap only

Decorate a circle of paper with patterns on both sides and cut out a spiral. Thread a piece of cotton through the centre and hang it over a radiator. The warm air rising will make the snake spin.

Spiral snakes

Air and music

Look for and listen to pieces of music associated with air and flight, wind and weather. Listen to recent pieces, such as: 'Up, up and away'; 'Red balloon'; 'Those magnificent men in their flying machines'. Collect together as many instruments as you can, and let the children sort them into those which need to have air blown through them in order to make the musical sound, and those which do not. Let the children handle the instruments in order to investigate for themselves how the sound is made.

Use **Copymaster 5** (Air and sounds) to record those instruments which are played by blowing air into them. The children are to draw a circle around those and colour them in.

Vibrations

Stretch an elastic band between the fingers and twang it to make a sound. The band vibrates when it moves back and forth quickly. Let the children feel their Adam's apple as they sing. They should be able to feel parts of their throats vibrate as they do so.

Make a sound catcher

Smooth some newspaper over one end of a cardboard tube and tape it in place. Sing down the tube and feel the paper at the same time. The sound sends vibrations through the air in the tube and this makes the paper shake. Kazoos work on the same principle, and if possible let the children play with some. They will really enjoy accompanying each other with their songs.

sound catcher

Sound vibrations

Blooter

Use a blooter and let the children investigate how the noise is made, and what they have to do to make high notes and lower notes.

blooter

33

Bottle music

Blow across the top of an empty bottle and see if it will make a sound. Put different amounts of water in the bottle and see if the sound changes. The more water there is in the bottle, the less air, and as smaller amounts of air vibrate more quickly, this makes a higher sound.

Musical pipes

Cut some artstraws® to different lengths and, starting with the shortest, lay them one by one on to a piece of sticky tape. Leave the longest straw till last.

Fix them in place by laying another piece of sticky tape over the first, then lift up the row of straws and blow gently across each straw. Find out which one makes the highest sound.

Mention that all sound needs air to be heard, and that in outer space, where there is no air, sound vibrations cannot be heard.

bottle music

musical pipes

DANCE, DRAMA, PE

DANCE

Wind movements

Talk about the way things move in the wind. In a gentle breeze, things move slowly and gracefully, bending, curling, rippling and waving. Contrast this with a storm, when things are being tossed about wildly this way and that. Ask the children to move as if they were being blown by the wind. Start off with calm, then change the pace to breeze, gale and storm.

Balloon movements

Take a balloon and blow it up. Ask the children to observe how it stretches and grows. Release the air slowly, and let the children see how the balloon grows smaller and smaller until it is just the same size as it was at first. Let the children explore stretching and curling in the same way as the balloon. Using a tambourine as accompaniment, the children can grow and stretch making wide shapes. They can then deflate and curl up in the same way as the balloon.

Blow up the balloon again, and this time let it go. Watch it fly around, twisting and turning as the air escapes. The children can try to move in this way also.

Finally, blow the balloon up and let it bounce gently across the floor. The children can try to follow this movement, and this may lead on to a discussion about the way birds fly through the air.

The children can then try to create movements to suggest soaring, gliding and swooping. They can think about the direction of their movement and also the level: low, medium and high. They can also include hops and jumps in this, to create a further impression of flight. Give lots of experience of these movements and let the children devise a simple sequence of movements linked with stretching and curling and including the directional movements at the different levels.

DRAMA

Improvise stories and adventures

Turn the role-play centre into an airport, or an aeroplane, and the children can be either passengers or crew. They can also make their own passports and tickets. They may try to relive their own experiences of holiday trips, or they might be like Indiana Jones on an exciting adventure.

Tell the story of 'The Sun and the Wind'. The children can try to improvise their own versions working with two other children, or as a small group with three members acting out the story for the rest.

RELIGIOUS EDUCATION

Talk about how all living things need air, and link this with discussions of God's wonderful world. Look for the wonders of creation, and talk about the weather which helps us to grow our food.

Talk about heaven, many people look up to the sky when they talk of God and heaven. Ask the children what their ideas of heaven are, and what God is like. Compare the ideas of children from different ethnic backgrounds. Find out about angels and other winged messengers from heaven.

HISTORY

True stories

Read stories of explorers sailing in ships powered by the wind, read about voyages of discovery, and man's early attempts to fly. Contrast these with fairy tales which have a flying theme, or are to do with epic journeys, and try to spot the difference between the two.

Talk about how in the past corn was ground, using windmills, and show the children photographs or drawings. If possible, try to visit a windmill to let the children see for themselves.

Tell the story of the Montgolfier Brothers' balloon flight, and see if the children can re-tell it. Try to show that this event would have been just as exciting as man's first rocket flight into space.

Aircraft and sailing vessels

Collect together as many illustrations and photographs as possible of aircraft, jets and rockets. Let the children try to sort them into chronological order. You can discuss their reasons with them. Do the same for sailing vessels, and try to include pictures of medieval boats,

eighteenth century sailing ships, tea-clippers like the *Cutty Sark*, and fast sailing yachts with their colourful spinnakers. Include also some pictures of the entrants in the tall ships race. The children may need to look for extra clues in these pictures since the style of the ships is old-fashioned, but some of them are only recently built. You can include here a discussion about pollution of the seas and how sail boats are generally much better for the environment.

Pictures of early hot-air balloons can be contrasted with some of the colourful and incredible shapes that we see today.

Moving with air

The children can colour the pictures on **Copymaster 6** (Moving with air), and then cut them out and place them in chronological order, from the earliest vehicles to the latest design. The top half of the sheet shows pictures of things moving with air through the *sky*, the bottom half is for those things which move with air over or through the *water*.

GEOGRAPHY

Aerial views

Watch videos of aerial flight and talk about how things look different when viewed from above. Some children who live in high-rise flats will be able to describe what things look like from high up. If possible, and with safety uppermost in mind, take the children to a high vantage point where they can look down on their surroundings. This vantage point can either be a building or a high hill. Look for observable features and places they recognise. Try to get hold of some aerial photographs of the area, and again look for those

things which are easily recognisable such as rivers and ponds, areas of woodland, fields and streets.

It is enough to be looking for these features at this stage, but you can start to introduce some geographical vocabulary such as slope, river, hill, wood, park and home, as recommended by the National Curriculum document. The children can try to devise their own symbols to represent each feature, and then try to draw a simple map of the local area or of a magical kingdom from one of their story-books.

Use **Copymaster 7** (Plans) to match the picture of an object with the plan or view of it as seen from above. The children are to draw a line from the picture to its plan, and then colour both of them the same colours so that the two match as closely as possible.

Weather record

The children can keep a daily weather record for a period of time, and you can devise a weather chart for this purpose.

A simple sheet can be drawn up, listing the days of the week and providing a set of appropriate symbols to indicate the type of weather on a particular day. If you prefer, let the children devise their own symbols. Have different groups of children record the weather over the period the topic runs, and at the end you can discuss which group kept the most detailed records.

Air 1

Moving air

Bunnycopter

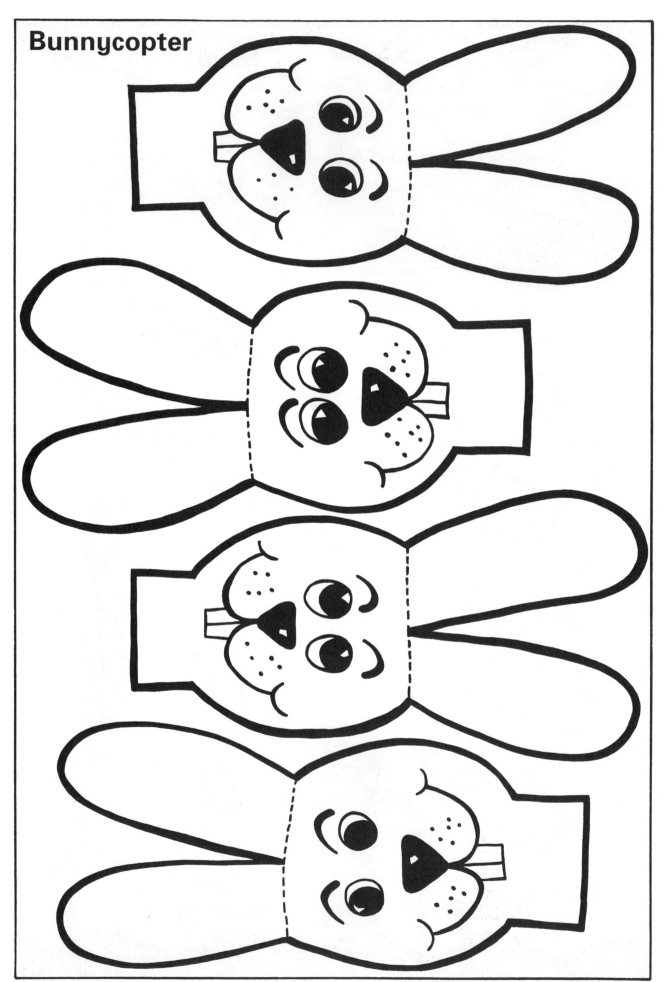

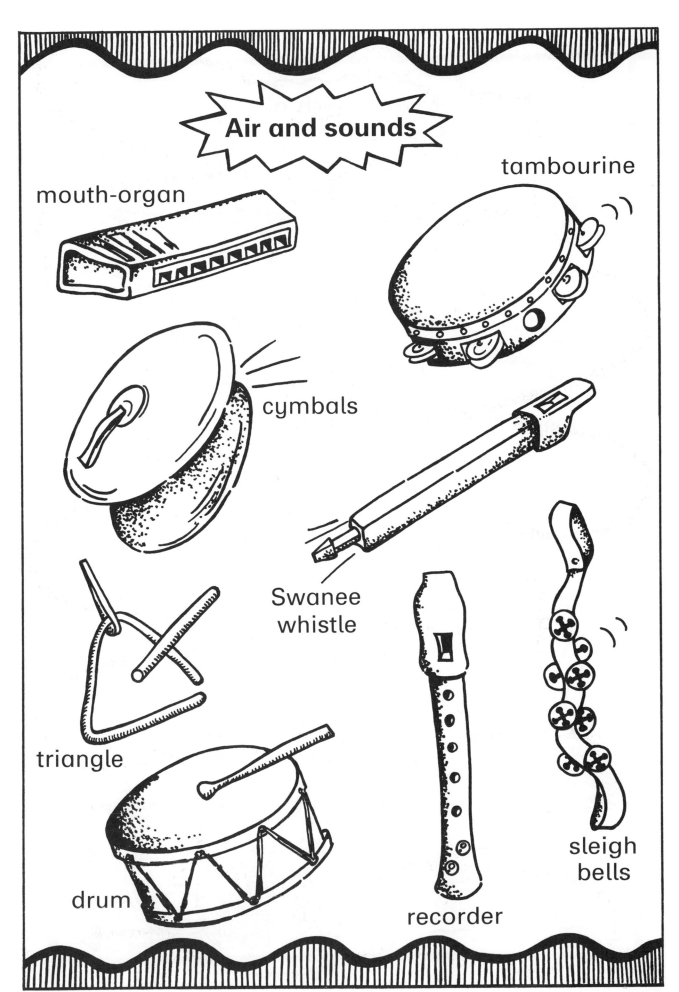

Air and sounds

mouth-organ

tambourine

cymbals

Swanee whistle

triangle

drum

recorder

sleigh bells

Moving with air

Plans

SCHOOL

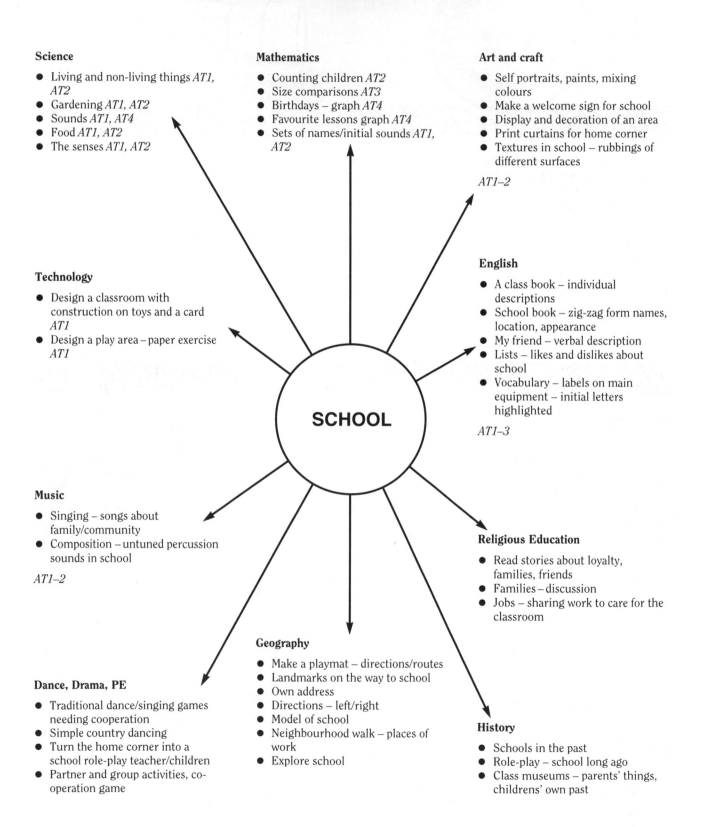

Science

- Living and non-living things *AT1, AT2*
- Gardening *AT1, AT2*
- Sounds *AT1, AT4*
- Food *AT1, AT2*
- The senses *AT1, AT2*

Technology

- Design a classroom with construction on toys and a card *AT1*
- Design a play area – paper exercise *AT1*

Music

- Singing – songs about family/community
- Composition – untuned percussion sounds in school

AT1–2

Dance, Drama, PE

- Traditional dance/singing games needing cooperation
- Simple country dancing
- Turn the home corner into a school role-play teacher/children
- Partner and group activities, co-operation game

Mathematics

- Counting children *AT2*
- Size comparisons *AT3*
- Birthdays – graph *AT4*
- Favourite lessons graph *AT4*
- Sets of names/initial sounds *AT1, AT2*

Geography

- Make a playmat – directions/routes
- Landmarks on the way to school
- Own address
- Directions – left/right
- Model of school
- Neighbourhood walk – places of work
- Explore school

Art and craft

- Self portraits, paints, mixing colours
- Make a welcome sign for school
- Display and decoration of an area
- Print curtains for home corner
- Textures in school – rubbings of different surfaces

AT1–2

English

- A class book – individual descriptions
- School book – zig-zag form names, location, appearance
- My friend – verbal description
- Lists – likes and dislikes about school
- Vocabulary – labels on main equipment – initial letters highlighted

AT1–3

Religious Education

- Read stories about loyalty, families, friends
- Families – discussion
- Jobs – sharing work to care for the classroom

History

- Schools in the past
- Role-play – school long ago
- Class museums – parents' things, childrens' own past

BASIC CONCEPTS

1 Most children in this country now go to school.

2 We go to school to learn.

3 We learn how to live with others and to make friends.

4 We learn about the world we live in.

5 We start school in the year we are five, and go until we are about 16. We can stay longer.

6 We go five days a week, but we have many holidays at home.

7 We usually go to a school near our home.

8 There are many adults in school who do different jobs to help run the place.

STARTING POINTS

● Take a walk round school and talk about what can be seen inside the grounds and immediately surrounding them. Try to find places in school which the children have never seen before.

● Take photographs of the new starters busy playing (or otherwise) on their first day at school, then look back at these later in the year to start the topic with a discussion of feelings.

● Visit another school in the neighbourhood and invite a return visit to spark off a discussion of similarities and differences.

● Turn the home corner into a mini-school, with small tables, a blackboard, paper, pencils and play equipment.

● If you have a video camera, or if a parent is willing to lend one, take some footage of different school activities being performed by the different age groups. Watch this to stimulate conversation about what kind of things go on in a school.

ENGLISH

Our class

Make a book about the class with a page for each child and the teacher. Discuss with the children how they now belong to a special group called a class, and what things will make their class special, for example behaviour, activities, appearance, and so on. Make the point about them being individuals in a group, and get each child to do a self-portrait for their page. You can then dictate or write something about what makes them special, such as their name, appearance, likes and dislikes.

Our school

Similarly, make a book about school, this time as a zig-zag book which can be displayed on a low surface for the children to look at. Include important conceptual details such as: our school's name; the location;

children are grouped in classes; there are adults in school with different jobs; the appearance of the building.

Use **Copymaster 1** (Cover sheet) as a cover for individual books about school, or as a general sheet on which the children can do writing or drawings. It can also be used as a sheet for handwriting practice. To highlight it as a lesson write, 'We learn to write in school'.

My friend

This can often be the most important thing to a child starting school. Try to identify a friend for everyone, even if you are that friend, or if they insist on one they play with at home. Talk about what things they like doing with the friend, and possibly find a friend or a group of friends for the playtime following the discussion. Some children need to be helped to make a friend. See *Blueprints Writing* for a copymaster sheet on this subject (My friend).

Likes and dislikes

Try to discuss what the children liked and disliked when they first started school and then later on, and again even a term later, to see if their perceptions have changed.

Use **Copymaster 2** (School) to record these details in list form, either individually or by enlarging to A3 size as a class exercise.

School vocabulary

As part of your work on spelling, label all the main items in the classroom and play I-spy to introduce initial sounds.

Use **Copymaster 3** (I-spy in school) as an exercise in identifying initial sounds.

MATHEMATICS

Counting

Use this opportunity to count the number of children in the class, the number of boys and girls, those absent and those present. Record the register in list form with

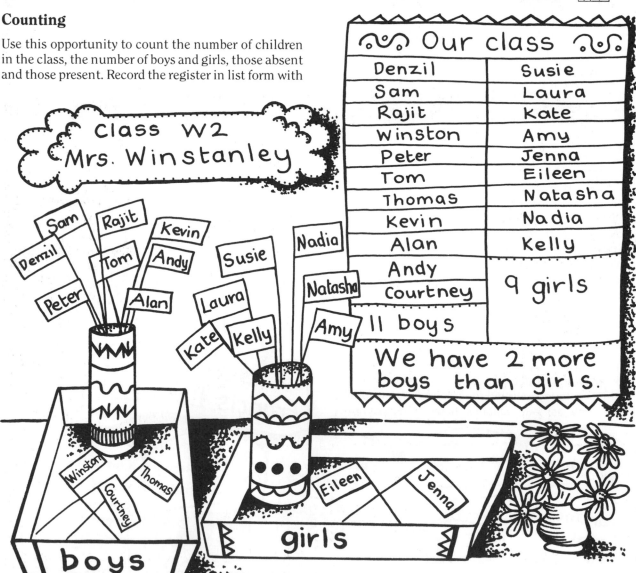

one column for boys and one for girls, with the total number at the bottom. Match the lines so that it can be seen at a glance which column has most and which least, and by how much.

Record the register each day in a practical form, having the children 'clock-on' by picking their name flag from a tray to put in the pot, thus leaving the flags of those absent in the tray. Count the quantities each day with the children.

Size

Look at size in the class, comparing height of children, height of tables and cupboards, length of tables and units, and width of these things too. You can also go round school and try to identify which rooms are the largest and smallest, which corridors are long and which short. Record with comparative vocabulary such as tall, tallest; small, smallest.

Birthdays

Find out if everyone knows their birthday and, if not, ask them to get their parents to help them learn the month and the date. This can be recorded on an on-going basis on a graph. Write everyone's name and the date of their birthday on a balloon shape, and put it in the correct month column. Then when the day arrives, add a star to the balloon to record visually the passing of time, the number of birthdays reached, and those still to come.

Katie

2nd.

enlargement

Birthday balloons

Favourite lessons and activities

As the mathematical conclusion to the discussions about likes and dislikes, record the favourite lessons and activities on a graph.

Use **Copymaster 4** (Favourite lessons) for the children to pick out their favourite activity and colour it in, as a contribution to the graph.

Sets of names

Identify the initial sound of everyone's first name and write them in sets of the same sound, counting the numbers which occur in each set. The names start with a capital, of course, and this is a useful opportunity to identify the capital form of the letter sounds.

CM5

SCIENCE

Living and non-living things

Go for a walk round school and try to find ten living and ten non-living things. It's best to restrict the number, or the list could be endless. Moreover, the children will feel a sense of achievement if they do find the required number. See *Blueprints Science Key Stage One*, Attainment Target 2, for further work on living and non-living things, including definitions.

Gardening

Find a small corner of the school, even if it is only a window-box, that can be improved by making a garden. Try to collect plants from parents, buy seedlings if possible, or grow annuals from seed. Let the children be responsible for maintenance of the area so that they have an input into the environment on behalf of the rest of school. Alternatively, they could take care of an

existing garden. In either case, this activity will contribute to the children's experience of living things.

Sounds

There are many different sounds in school, not least the children's own voices. Go on a walk round school to discover the variety. This is a good exercise in listening and aural discrimination.

Use **Copymaster 5** (Sounds in school) to record these sounds, and for the children to attempt to order sounds by volume.

Food in school

Discuss the kinds of food the children like, and the type of food they eat in school at different times of the day. For example, if they bring snacks, how many have sweets, chocolate and flavoured crisps, and how many have a more healthy snack such as fruit? Talk about lunch and the types of food brought as a packed lunch and the variety of school meals available. Identify the foods which are good for general health and teeth.

Make a graph of the favourite types of snack food, using the empty packets as the elements of the graph. Alternatively, cut out large and small circles of paper to represent plates and bowls, and ask the children to draw in their favourite school lunch or packed lunch. Display these on a chequered background like a table-cloth.

Ask the children to record pictorially, or in list form, the things they eat at different times of the day.

Observation with all the senses

Walk round school to make a general observation with all the senses: sight, hearing, touch, smell and, if possible, taste. If you have a kitchen, the cook may be able to help here. Brief the children beforehand, and record for yourself general observations that will later help the children decide which thing they remember from each sensory area.

After the walk, get the children to record their observations in simple sentences, writing down what they sensed and where, e.g., 'I saw a litter-bin. It was in the playground'.

TECHNOLOGY

Design a classroom

Use an assortment of construction bricks and shapes, and a designated floor area on which the children can design a classroom layout in a practical 3D way. Give them some scissors and paper which they can use to make carpets or large table-tops. The bricks can represent different types of furniture, or be used to make partitions or closed areas. Give them some Lego® people to test the room.

Design a play area

Children sometimes find the playground rather an empty place and would like some outdoor play equipment. In some schools with a nursery unit, the children can see such equipment being used by the lucky inhabitants. Discuss what sort of play equipment the children have used in parks, and other places, and which they think will be suitable for school, and why. Go outside and look at the space available and then try to measure out the space a swing or climbing-frame might take, using the children themselves as units of measurement.

Some children like to sit quietly in the playground with a friend. Ask the children to consider such a rest area.

Use the children as units of measurement.

ART AND CRAFT

Self-portraits

Ask everyone in class to draw or paint a self-portrait, using a mirror for observation of details. Encourage the children to match eye and hair colour as exactly as possible, by mixing paint or selecting a colour from the great variety available in wax crayons.

Cut out the portraits and mount them as an 'Our class' montage.

child's painting cut out

Welcome to our school

Make a sign

Make a welcome sign for the entrance hall, discussing beforehand the sort of decoration and style that might be appropriate, and the size and materials to be used. Two or three children might be able to cooperate to produce a large sign with a collection of drawn flowers, for example, as decoration.

Display and decoration

Consult the children when setting up a new reading corner, a change for the home corner, a seasonal display, or a curricular display. Discuss what elements are needed, what colours to use, size and location. This is a good discussion exercise as well as being an excellent introduction to aesthetic design. As part of this aspect, point out different displays round school to encourage observation.

Curtains

If you, or another class, need new curtains or cushion covers for the home corner, get the children to print the fabric. Use old cotton sheets and a mix of two parts PVA glue to one part powder paint. A bold design may then be printed with scrap items such as cardboard tube ends, sponge shapes, and potato shapes. Let the children decide on the shapes, colours and design. This printed fabric won't be washable, but you can use fabric paints as the printing medium if a longer life is needed.

home corner

curtains

cushion covers

Textures in school

Make a textural record of a walk round school using an assortment of medium quality papers and a variety of thick wax crayons to take rubbings of different surfaces. For example, paths, walls, carpets, wood, manhole covers, trees, toys such as Lego® boards, and other linked yet flat surfaces. The youngest children need help to keep the paper in position and to apply the correct amount of pressure with the crayons. Mount these rubbings as a puzzle to match the name of the surface with the correct picture.

make jigsaws

tree bark

hall carpet

floor tiles

What are these surfaces?

① tree bark ② carpet ③ wallpaper ④ bricks
⑤ hall floor ⑥ leaf ⑦ wooden gate

Where did we find these surfaces in our school?

Textures in school

51

Sing songs

There are many songs about working together which best illustrate how we would like life at school to be. They are the songs about community and helping each other. The children may already know some songs and be able to make suggestions about suitable ones. For example: 'Girls and boys come out to play'; 'Mary had a little lamb'; 'Here we go round the mulberry bush'; 'The farmer's in his den'. *Someone's singing Lord* (A. & C. Black) is a useful anthology of songs, including: 'At half past three we go home to tea'; 'The ink is black, the page is white'; 'Oh Jesus we are well and strong'.

Sounds all right

As part of the work on sounds in the Science section, try to identify five different sounds which are heard often in your school, then find some of the non-tuned percussion instruments to represent these sounds. For example, footsteps across the hall floor could be portrayed by taps with the rhythm sticks (wooden batons) or children's voices in the playground by shaken tambourine, and so on.

When they have been selected, make up a pattern of these sounds into a school sounds song.

Design some symbols for the different instruments and write down a simple score to indicate how many times the sound is played in the song and when. As the children get used to this, the pattern can be played two or three times to make the song.

School sounds song

DANCE

Try traditional dance games which have a voice accompaniment and involve the children working together, for example: 'Ring a ring of roses'; 'Here we go round the mulberry bush'; 'In and out the fairy bluebells'; 'The farmer's in his den'; 'Lucy Locket lost her pocket'.

The simple country dances which require counting of steps are more suitable for older children, but this age group could have great fun doing parts of the dances involving joined hands in a circle, skipping round holding hands with a partner, or dancing round on the spot with a partner.

DRAMA

Turn the home corner into a school. This could be a modern school or a very old one such as a dame-school. For the latter you will need some small blackboards for slates, chalks, some shawls and flat hats for the children and a long skirt for the dame. Whichever type of school you choose, give the children some suggestions for the otherwise free role-play. For example, one child could be naughty, one could be late, one could do specially good work or help someone. Watch to see how the children work out these situations – usually in terms of your own teaching style!

PE

Play partner activities such as mirrors, three-legged walking and group games such as Follow my leader, Simon says, and so on. There is now a new group co-operation toy on the market which is a very light parachute sheet operated by a group of children – lifted into the air by all the arms moving upwards together, and down by their downwards movement. Many games can be devised such as alternate children in the circle letting go when the parachute is up and running into the centre, then back to their place to take over as the others do the same.

Read stories

There are many stories about people: helping each other, loyalty, sharing, and families, all of which contribute to the ethos of a good school. Well-known modern stories include: 'The little red hen', who wanted everyone to work together, and *Tyrone the dirty rotten cheat* by Hans Wilhelm (Hippo), where the rest of the dinosaur friends work together to make their camp happy despite Tyrone.

Families

See the topic on 'Family' for further ideas, and for this aspect of the curriculum talk about how the class and the school are a kind of family. You may be able to decide together on some rules and aspirations for your class 'family'. For example, 'Our class is kind to others, looks after all living things, keeps the classroom tidy'.

Jobs

Let the children help each other and contribute to the smooth organisation of the classroom by taking turns at a variety of jobs like tidying the tables, sharpening the pencils, putting straws in the milk, watering the plants and so on.

Encourage everyone to do their own bit towards keeping the cloakroom and lunch boxes and other communal areas tidy. The main point is that we need to begin to take on responsibility for the place we live in and life we lead, even at this early age. This is done by learning to care for others.

Jobs in the classroom

Schools in the past

If you have a local heritage centre with an old school room (usually Victorian) a visit would spark off much discussion about the relative merits of this and your own school. Talk about the similarities and differences.

Time travel

Turn your classroom into an old school for the day. Use pictorial evidence such as photographs to help design the room. Schools from the 1960s or Victorian times are sufficiently different to facilitate comparison, and may have been attended by mature parents and grand-parents. Rearrange the tables for the day, and possibly arrange for the children to wear similar clothes to the children of the period and do some of the activities of the time such as writing the alphabet, counting out

loud, singing, outdoor games and PE. It is important to relate the time period to something the children know, such as a parent's experience, or even your own school-days.

Class museum

Ask the children to bring in something from their parents' or grandparents' school-days. It could be an old school hat, bag, tie or an exercise book; a class photograph or the dreaded School Report Card (with teacher's comments)!

From the children's own school past, make a similar museum with items from nursery, playgroup, work from the previous year in your school or even the early work from the present class. It is always enlightening to look back to the front of the present writing book to see, 'How I used to do stories'.

Class museum

Make a playmat

To give practice in map form and in following directions, give the children a large sheet of paper and help them to make a playmat like those commercially produced. It could be of any of the following: a farm with fields, paths, tracks and buildings; a town with roads, houses, factories, schools; a harbour with railway lines, water, roads.

These can be coloured in and played with with small vehicles. Introduce directions into the play with suggestions such as: 'Can you drive to the hospital?'; 'Who can find the shortest way to the shops from the school?'; 'Tell me how to get to school'; 'Here's my house'.

Use **Copymaster 6** (Routes) which is a simple tracking exercise to train the eye to scan the page for details. The children can draw in details such as houses, hospital, park and other features in their own neighbourhood, and then draw with a coloured pencil the route they want to take from their imaginary home to school. They can add paths across grassed areas to make the route shorter.

The way home

Talk about the route the children take from their own home to school. What sort of things do they see on the way? Do they see the same people regularly engaged in the same jobs, such as the postman, the milkman, the lollipop lady/man? What kind of buildings do they pass on the way? Are there houses, shops, factories, or open spaces such as a park, fields, waste-ground? Try to get them to describe the route verbally in very simple terms, 'I go down the road, turn the corner, go past the newsagent's and round the corner to school'.

Direction may be beyond most children at this level, but you can introduce it as in the following activity. Use **Copymaster 7** (On my way to school) which shows a simple route on to which the children can add details of things they actually see on their route to school.

My address

As part of the work on the previous activity, help the children to learn their own address and telephone number if applicable. Get them to write this down on a decorated card to keep for personal reference.

Direction

Play at changing direction in the hall or the playground, with you giving instructions (e.g. 'Turn left, right, opposite way, back up') to the children as radio-controlled cars. A useful aide-mémoire is to give them something to hold in the right hand. If any of the children have a radio-controlled car or a programmable toy, you could devise short routes which they can follow, such as, 'Straight ahead, turn left, left again'.

A model school

Make a model of school, using cardboard boxes. At this level it need not be strictly to scale, but you can help the children to observe the size differences of parts of the building from outside, such as the garden shed and the main hall. Try to find different places where the whole building can be seen and get the children to draw it from these different viewpoints and construct the model from these drawings. Use lumps of foam or balls of wool for trees and bushes, walls from Newclay, hills from screwed up paper, fences from balsa wood, and so on.

A neighbourhood walk

Go for a walk round the immediate neighbourhood of the school to see how many places of work there are, then record these findings pictorially or as a picture graph or a frieze.

Don't forget to include recreational facilities such as the swimming pool or sports centre, where people also work. Include other schools and places of worship, where even if the religious officials are sometimes unpaid, there may be paid caretakers.

Explore school

Go for regular short walks round school, either in small groups or as a class, letting the children take turns at guiding the group, 'Today, Susie can show us the way to the staffroom'. This will help the children become familiar with the building, and help them to build confidence as they get to know their way around.

Places where people work near school

St. Ann's church — the newsagent — John's place the garage — Smith and Sons. the cotton factory — Taylor Park — Men work Victoria road

school

Things I like about school.

Things I don't like about school.

I-spy in school

t □ □ □ □

p □ □ □ □ □

b □ □ □ □

t □ □ □

p □ □ □ □

| books | paint | table | pencil | toys |

Favourite lessons

Once upon a time...

Sounds in school

Which sound was loudest?   Number it **1**.
Which sound was softest?   Number it **6**.
Put the sounds in order on the table below.

		Number
	door banging	
	children talking	
	feet walking	

Routes

Find the way to school.

home

school

PROTECTION

Science

- Safety in school *AT1, AT2*
- Protecting the body from disease *AT1, AT2*
- Make a health centre *AT1, AT2*
- Research on plant and animal protection *AT1, AT2*
- Feeding birds *AT1, AT2*
- Model animals *AT1, AT2*
- Car safety *AT1, AT2, AT4*
- First-aid *AT1, AT2*
- Protective clothes *AT1, AT2*

Mathematics

- Graphs *AT1, AT4*

Art and craft

- Collage of plants and animals colours and patterns
- Fashion design for safety
- Shell patterns
- Camouflage designs
- Puppets for road safety
- Treasure-chests

AT1–2

Technology

- Build a castle *AT2*
- Build a bird table *AT2*
- Make a drawbridge *AT2*
- Imaginary designs *AT1*

English

- Read stories
- Imaginative writing
- Posters

AT1–3

PROTECTION

Music

- Lullabies – listening
- Composition

AT1–2

Religious Education

- Discuss and read stories of Noah's Ark, Nativity, Good Samaratin
- Learn Green Cross Code
- Poisons and drugs

Dance, Drama, PE

- Role-play, ad lib – stories from RE
- Mime – home care
- Dance – animal defence
- Swimming
- Self-defence

Geography

- Looking after the neighbourhood
- Safety on the road
- Animals in danger
- Bottle world

History

- Castles
- Protecting homes
- Police
- Armed forces

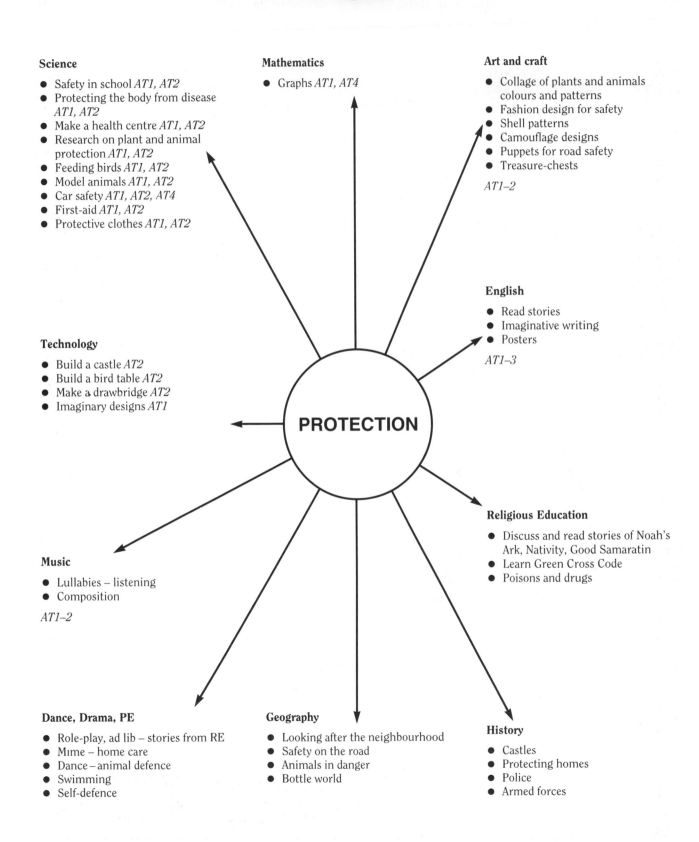

63

1 Everyone must learn to protect themselves from dangers.

2 Humans sometimes need protective clothing.

3 We need to protect our homes and families.

4 Animals protect their young and their territory.

5 We must all work together to protect our local environment and the whole world.

STARTING POINTS

● Put up a display of protective clothing from a variety of different hobbies and occupations. This could include goggles, helmets, shin-pads, jackets and suits, footwear and gloves. The children themselves and local organisations may be willing to lend items ranging from diving masks, cricket gloves, shin protectors and skateboard pads, to fireman's helmets or miner's boots.

● You could start off with swimming equipment such as armbands, floats, rings, goggles, masks and so on.

● Ask the local constabulary Road Safety Team to do a road safety session in school. Many have very enter-taining puppet shows and other visual aids, and use role-play to get the message across.

● Watch a wildlife video showing animals protecting their young or the group. Look also at the way animals use camouflage and armour to protect themselves.

● Visit a castle or a fortified village and get the feel of the defences at first-hand by walking the battlements and peeping through slit windows.

● Similarly, arrange a visit to a fire station to look at the protective clothing and rescue equipment. The video of 'Fireman Sam' is also a good introduction to this topic.

ENGLISH

Read stories

Read stories which have a strong element of protection in them. For example, 'The three little pigs' are trying to protect themselves from the wolf; 'Fireman Sam' helps to keep Pontypandy safe; 'The seven dwarves' try to protect Snow White from the Wicked Queen, and so on.

Write stories

Discuss possible story lines that include some aspect of protection, i.e. someone saved, something protected from damage or theft. You and the children can decide on the characters, the setting, the main event and the ending. Possible themes could include: a snail who

lost his shell; a sea rescue; the night we had a burglar; saving our pond; preventing a road accident; a fire at school.

Make posters

Posters use a different type of language from that which is found in narrative. On the whole, titles, phrases and short sentences are used. For the purposes of this topic, you could make warning or informative posters to be put up in school or around the neighbourhood. Topics could include any of the following: cleaning teeth and other aspects of hygiene; road safety; stranger danger; safety and electricity; saving water; safe cycling clothes.

Look at published posters to get an idea of the style, content, type of language, artwork and size, and then discuss your own poster collection. Decide who the audience is, and which subject or subjects in this topic you wish to highlight. Let the children draw rough copies first so that you can help them with layout and language. Vocabulary needs to be short and snappy to catch the attention. Discuss use of words and phrases such as: stop, wait, look out, stay safe, help needed.

Use **Copymaster 1** (Cover sheet) as a base for a poster or for writing vocabulary on. Letters to parents about visits in conjunction with this topic can also be written on this sheet. It may also be used for any stories or for a topic book cover.

MATHEMATICS

Graphs

The children need to learn how to collect, process and interpret data. To give them practice in this, it is useful to undertake surveys recorded in graphs and charts. Organise surveys to find out any of the following information: the number of children in school or the class who own cycle helmets; the number of children who have fluorescent strips on coats; the number of times a day children clean teeth and have a bath or a wash; the number of children who know the Green Cross Code.

Use **Copymaster 2** (Car safety) to organise a graph to show how many parents have safety features in their cars. You will also need to find out how many parents have cars and do not have the safety features. Try to get the children to use both pieces of information and hypothesise. What would happen if the cars without the safety features for children were involved in an accident? The pictures are the elements of the graph and can be cut up and coloured in.

You can use a tally sheet to collect the information before recording it on the graph.

Use a tally sheet to collect information.

65

Safety in school

Go for a walk round school and look out for safety features such as sockets not overloaded and cooker switched off at the mains. At the same time, note unsafe things such as tight springs on doors and smelly drains. Discuss with the children how these things might be improved. Money will have to come into the discussion! You can make a class list of improvements needed and tick them off if they get done.

Protecting the body from illness and disease

See the topic on 'My body' for some ideas. You may feel you need to give practical demonstrations on some aspects of health care and you can use dolls to show children how to wash body and hair. Dental firms often give free samples of toothbrushes and toothpaste and you can have a cleaning session in class. You will obviously try to encourage habits of personal hygiene during the day as part of normal routine.

Talk about germs and the effect they have on us. Hold an imaginative drawing session where the children must draw the most awful germ they can imagine and say what it does to the body!

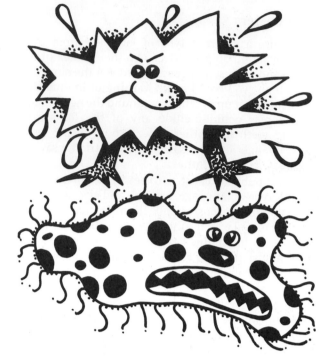

Awful germs!

1kg. melted lard
1kg. mixed rabbit food
Chopped up apple
bacon rind
½ kg. bird peanuts
Mix all dry ingredients
with lard and put in
mould until set.

mixture in here

50 cm string

knot

margarine tub

Make a bird cake.

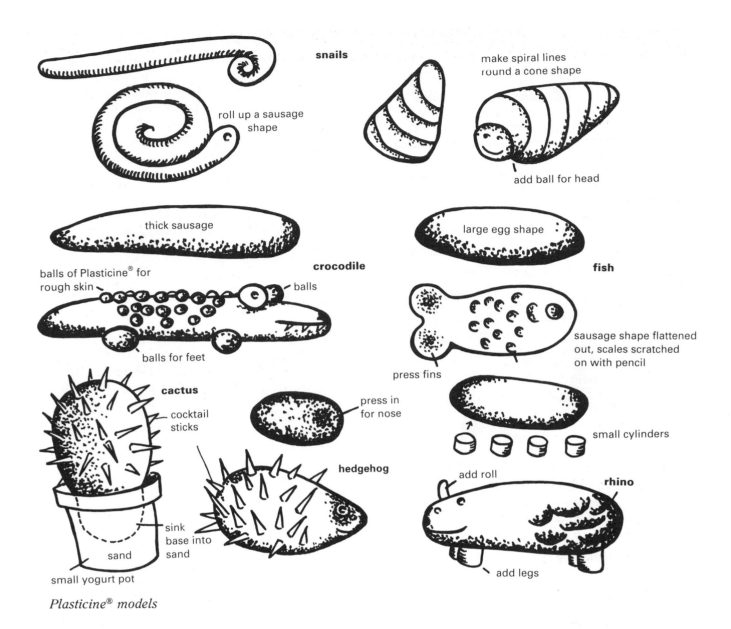

snails

make spiral lines round a cone shape

roll up a sausage shape

add ball for head

thick sausage

large egg shape

balls of Plasticine® for rough skin

crocodile

balls

fish

balls for feet

sausage shape flattened out, scales scratched on with pencil

press fins

cactus

cocktail sticks

press in for nose

small cylinders

hedgehog

add roll

rhino

sink base into sand

sand

small yogurt pot

add legs

Plasticine® models

Make a health centre

Turn the home corner into a health centre. Put health care posters up and notices about immunisations, healthy foods, dental visits and baby clinics. You can use dolls as patients. The accent in this unit should be on prevention of illness.

Look at plants and animals

Watch wildlife videos showing camouflage and other protective features, territorial habits, protection of young, and protective devices on plants such as spikes and thorns. Take the children to the library to find animal books and help them look through to find relevant pictures. Copying pictures can be a useful exercise to teach the children close observation of detail.

Use **Copymaster 3** (Camouflage) to show how an animal's colour can help hide it from predators or from prey. The children are to colour the animals and their habitat, using books or pictures as reference.

Bird cake

Wild birds sometimes need a little extra food in the winter, so make bird cake to provide them with some of the foods that are difficult to find.

Make Plasticine® models

Use Plasticine® and Play-Doh® to make models of animals and plants to show protective features like spines, scales, gnarled skin, horns and shells.

Make cardboard tube animals

Use cardboard tubes from household products as the base of the body and add card head and legs as shown. Cover the backs of the animals with different fabrics to be wool, fur or blubbery skin, all of which help keep the animal's body temperature even. Use foam sheets, fur fabric, wool waste, cotton-wool and feathers.

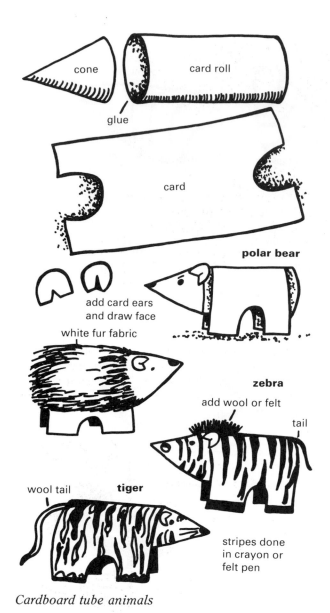

cone

card roll

glue

card

add card ears
and draw face

polar bear

white fur fabric

zebra

add wool or felt

tail

wool tail　　**tiger**

stripes done
in crayon or
felt pen

Cardboard tube animals

Look at seat-belts

Look at how seat-belts and child seats fit in a car, and how they hold a person in place. If possible, let the children have direct experience of this. Contact ROSPA (Royal Society for the Prevention of Accidents) and car manufacturers for video material showing accident situations with seat-belts and dummies.

First-aid

Ask the Ambulance Service to send someone to school to talk to the children about first-aid. Even very young children can be shown the recovery position and how to keep a person warm, not move them, and call for help to protect the casualty from getting worse. You can have a few accidents in a role-play situation.

Protective clothes

Make a display of the protective clothes used for hobbies and work. Try to arrange a visit from the Fire-Brigade and look at the clothes the fire-fighters wear.

Let the children try on the clothes and equipment in your display and talk about which parts of the body are protected from what danger. See how many different types of protective gear you can find for one part of the body, for example the head.

Use **Copymaster 4** (Clothes for protection) to link clothes to body parts. The children have to read the words (there are picture clues) and match clothes to parts of the body by writing the appropriate word.

Use **Copymaster 5** (Protect your body) for the children to draw on the protective clothes they may need for any one activity. This can be as ordinary as going out in the rain. See the first topic book in this series, *Blueprints Topics 5–8*, for a whole topic on 'Clothes'.

TECHNOLOGY ▶

Make a castle

Use Lego®, Duplo®, wooden bricks or large cardboard boxes to build a castle. Castles were designed to be strong enough to protect inhabitants from all invaders. Make the special teaching points of the exercise wall-building with interlocking bricks, and creating a broad base for stability. If you use cardboard boxes and want to stick them together, investigate the best glues to use.

Build a bird table

Discuss the design for the table based on where it is to be sited. This will determine whether it can be free-standing or hanging, and what size it will be. Talk about the materials needed for strength, weather-proof

quality and cost. It may need a rim round the edge to stop food falling off, or it may need some sort of baffle to prevent cats from climbing up. The children may want to build in some sort of camouflage for extra protection.

To plan out the design you will find a draft sheet useful. You may use **Copymaster 5** (Draft sheet) from the topic on 'My body' (p. 117) for this purpose.

Make a drawbridge for a castle

If you have a toy castle or have made a model one (see the topic on 'Buildings') you can make a drawbridge using balsa wood or card. The two main design features to discuss are the hinge for the base of the bridge, and the hoist mechanism.

A hanging bird table

Imaginary designs

Draw up imaginary designs for any of the following items which all need a strong protective element in them: a pet hutch for the garden; a safe playground for your school; a safety suit for a journey to the moon, the shops, the jungle; a safe house for an old person, blind person, person with a wheelchair or a toddler.

Use the draft sheet mentioned above to plan out your design.

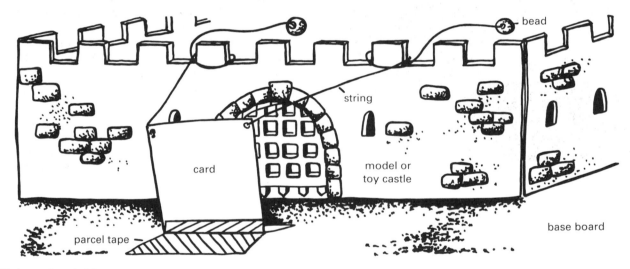

Make a drawbridge.

ART AND CRAFT

Collage

Use a variety of materials to create a butterfly, bird or flower which has colours designed to repel a potential enemy. Perhaps the butterfly could have huge eye patterns on its wings to imitate a bird. The flower might have long spikes coming from the centre. All that is necessary is that the children keep the brief in mind as they make their picture and choose colours and materials accordingly.

Fashion design

Use felt tips or paints to draw coats and other garments that can be seen at night. Fluorescent pens and paints are now readily available. Ask the children to use these as part of the design of the fabric, but not to use them exclusively.

Print shell patterns

Shells protect the soft bodies of many sea and land creatures, including snails and crabs. Use Newclay to make printing blocks showing shell designs. Make circular, linear or spiral designs on a variety of papers.

69

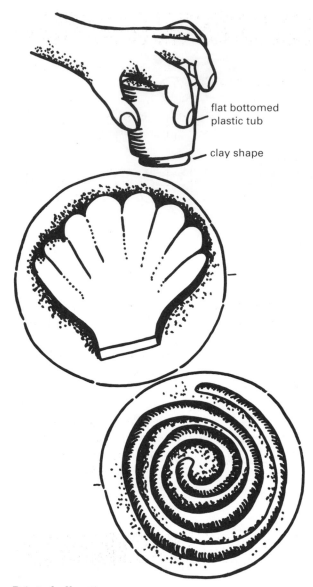

flat bottomed
plastic tub

clay shape

Print shell patterns.

Camouflage colours

Use paints to paint different camouflage designs such as a tiger or zebra stripes, or the design used on military vehicles. Note that the colours for snow camouflage are different from those used for green terrain.

Puppets

See the topic 'My body' for ideas for puppets and use them to make up your own road safety puppet show.

Treasure-chests

Make imaginary treasure-chests by decorating hinged margarine tubs with paint. Mix PVA glue with the paint to make it stick to the plastic. You can then stick on old buckles, bits of belts, coloured cellophane®, buttons or glitter. Talk about what the children classify as treasure. It might be small toys and trinkets, bits of shell and string, or even sweets.

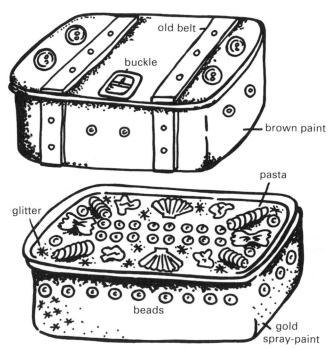

old belt

buckle

brown paint

pasta

glitter

beads

gold
spray-paint

Treasure-chests

MUSIC

Lullabies

Talk to the children about what sort of songs make them feel warm, safe, and well-protected from the world. They may come up with a variety of unusual songs for many different reasons, and some of these may be bedtime lullabies. Make a class collection of lullabies and write out the words on large sheets of paper. The children can then do illustrations round each one. Make these into a book which other classes could read and add to later.

Make up songs

Using simple well known tunes such as, 'London's burning', or 'Frère Jacques', make up words to go with them about any of the main themes in this topic. The children will be able to help. For example, to 'London's burning' you could try:

Make the world green, make the world green,
Plant a tree now, plant a tree now,
Grow well, grow tall,
Keep our world green, keep our world green.

Such songs are fun to sing and easy to remember. The children should also enjoy their contribution.

DANCE, DRAMA, PE

DANCE

Movement with percussion

Talk about how animals protect their young and then, using non-tuned percussion instruments to accompany movement, work out a short episode, for example showing a lion attack on a herd of wildebeest. Talk about how each of the animals would move: stalking, panicked flight or strong defence, and which instruments best accompany each movement. They may like the rickrack to be a danger sound or drums for attack and defence.

DRAMA

Role-play

Use role-play to go over the Green Cross Code, using children as cars and pedestrians, and marking out road boundaries on the hall floor.

Ad lib

Act out well-known bible stories such as, The good Samaritan, Noah's ark or the Nativity. You can read the stories and help the children to represent the various characters in an ad lib situation. Encourage the children to say what they think the characters would say. For example, what would the Samaritan say to the wounded man, or what would Joseph say to the inn-keeper?

Mime

Mime the various activities involved in keeping a home such as cleaning, decorating, gardening, making repairs, locking up for the night.

PE

Swimming

If possible, go swimming as part of your PE programme but if not, encourage the children to go with parents by showing posters and equipment and explaining the importance for personal safety as well as pleasure.

Self-defence

If there are any children in school who belong to a self-defence club for karate or one of the other disciplines, get them to give a demonstration and show equipment to the children. It is important to explain the defensive and disciplined nature of such activities.

RELIGIOUS EDUCATION

Read stories

Read the stories of The good Samaritan, the Nativity, Noah's ark, and talk about the protective elements in the stories (see the Drama section). The parable of the talents is also a good story for this topic as it shows that we must learn to look after ourselves and make the most of our attributes.

The Green Cross Code

Based on the principle that we must look after ourselves, learn the Green Cross Code and get the children to help each other as you act out the Code. Ask the children to make posters to teach others the Code.

Poisons

Medicines, drugs, wild berries, toadstools and alcohol can all be harmful to the body. You could try getting this important message across by telling the children of the dangers to their bodies and asking them to help younger or less aware children understand these dangers. This could be done with posters or written messages round school, or by role-playing a situation where a child has eaten some toadstools and is sick.

HISTORY

Castles and armour

Ask the children to bring in toy knights in armour and, if possible, a castle. Collect books and pictures showing fortifications of different kinds such as fortified villages and towns as well as castles from all over the world.

Have a go at making a castle. Pay particular attention to the defensive features such as the walls, portcullis and drawbridge. You will also need to discuss what danger the people wished to protect themselves from.

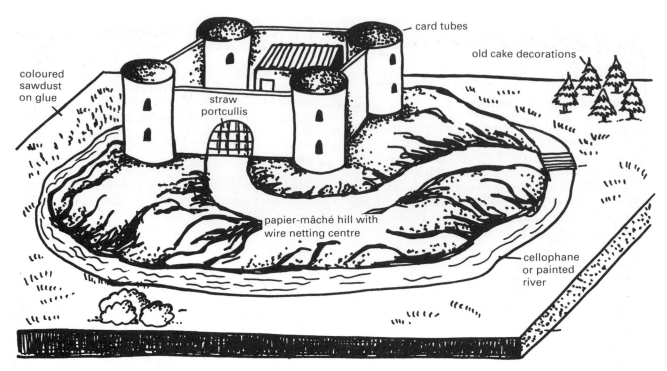

Model castle

Use **Copymaster 6** (A safe place) which shows a landscape with several places that a castle could be sited on to afford best protection. The children have to decide where they think is best and draw the castle there. The picture can also be coloured in.

Protecting our homes

Look at how we protect our homes. Ask the children to look for protective devices in their homes such as locks, double-glazing, security cameras and burglar alarms, gates, walls and fences. They can make a list with their parents help and then you can collate this material into graph form. Look at another aspect of protection by home maintenance; painting, pointing, rewiring, replumbing with non-lead pipes, double-glazing and so on.

Police

Use books to show how the police came into existence, and ask the local community policeman to come into school to talk casually to the children about how everyone can help towards the care of the community. This may be an over-sensitive issue in some schools, so you must use your own discretion to decide whether a visit would be counter-productive.

The armed forces

If you work in a Service school, or if some children in your class have parents in the armed forces, you could ask one of them to come in to talk to the children, wearing their uniform. Look at pictures, toys and models of soldiers from the past. Watch videos of state occasions to see the military guard. You may live near enough to London to watch the Changing of the Guard at the Palace.

GEOGRAPHY

Looking after the neighbourhood

Go for a walk round school or the local neighbourhood to look at how well it is being cared for.

Use **Copymaster 7** (Protecting our environment) to make a tally of the features you find. The children may be able to help with litter collection or gardening in school, and they can talk to the caretaker about the main problems in keeping the school well cared for.

If possible, get the children involved in a local conservation project which could be anything from repairing dry-stone walling, pond reclamation and litter removal from an old railway cutting, to helping to make a small nature reserve. The National Trust may have information about local projects, or indeed your own local council may be able to help.

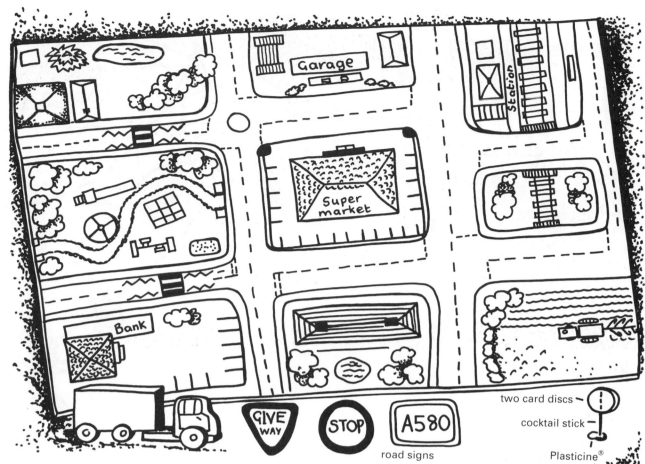

Road mat

Safety on the road

Look at road signs and how they help prevent accidents by guiding and controlling traffic. Make small signs for use on a play road mat with toy cars.

Animals in danger

Watch videos of wildlife and make a display of toy animals, using the species which are in danger of extinction. Write to the World Wildlife Fund to ask for posters and information about activities which the children can be involved in.

A bottle world

Make a bottle garden to give the children an idea of how the world and its atmosphere are almost like a bottle, with the contents recycling and regenerating. You can talk about what happens when poisonous gases and effluent are poured out into the globe. Put small houses or little plastic figures such as Lego® in the bottle to make it into a model world. See the topic on 'Dinosaurs' for use of a bottle garden to show the water cycle.

Protection 1

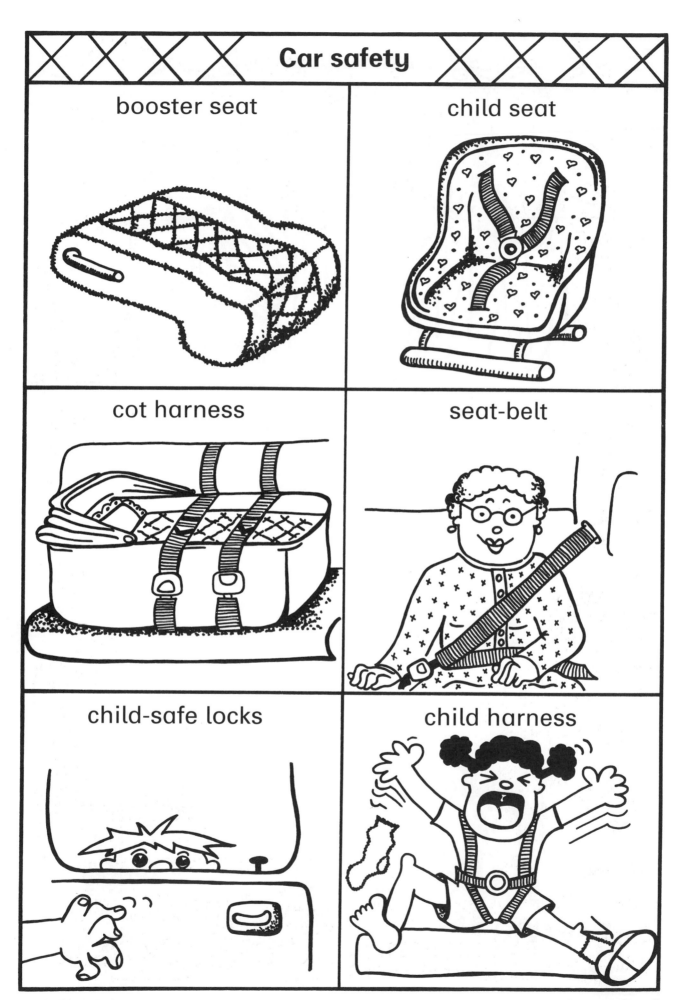

Car safety

booster seat

child seat

cot harness

seat-belt

child-safe locks

child harness

Camouflage

Clothes for protection

Which part of your body do these things protect?

helmet

goggles

boots

gloves

kagool

		are protected by
hands		
head		
body		
eyes		
feet		

Protect your body

You are dressing for a hobby,
or to start a job.
What do you need to wear?

A safe place

Draw your castle where it will be best protected.

Protecting our environment

litter-bins	large trees
bushes	copses and woods
hedges	fences
sweeping of paths, roads and yards	gardening
repairing and painting	

FIRE

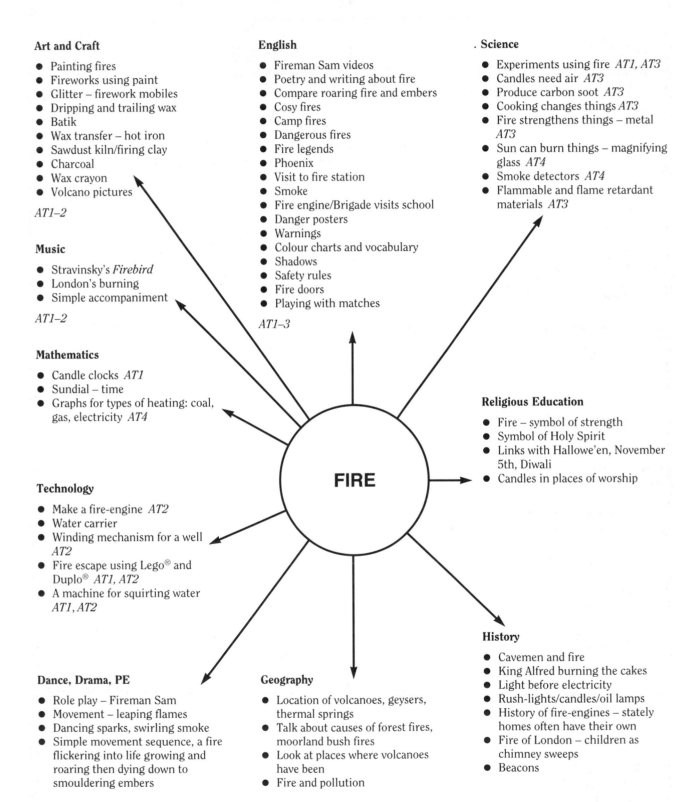

Art and Craft

- Painting fires
- Fireworks using paint
- Glitter – firework mobiles
- Dripping and trailing wax
- Batik
- Wax transfer – hot iron
- Sawdust kiln/firing clay
- Charcoal
- Wax crayon
- Volcano pictures

AT1–2

Music

- Stravinsky's *Firebird*
- London's burning
- Simple accompaniment

AT1–2

Mathematics

- Candle clocks *AT1*
- Sundial – time
- Graphs for types of heating: coal, gas, electricity *AT4*

Technology

- Make a fire-engine *AT2*
- Water carrier
- Winding mechanism for a well *AT2*
- Fire escape using Lego® and Duplo® *AT1, AT2*
- A machine for squirting water *AT1, AT2*

Dance, Drama, PE

- Role play – Fireman Sam
- Movement – leaping flames
- Dancing sparks, swirling smoke
- Simple movement sequence, a fire flickering into life growing and roaring then dying down to smouldering embers

English

- Fireman Sam videos
- Poetry and writing about fire
- Compare roaring fire and embers
- Cosy fires
- Camp fires
- Dangerous fires
- Fire legends
- Phoenix
- Visit to fire station
- Smoke
- Fire engine/Brigade visits school
- Danger posters
- Warnings
- Colour charts and vocabulary
- Shadows
- Safety rules
- Fire doors
- Playing with matches

AT1–3

Geography

- Location of volcanoes, geysers, thermal springs
- Talk about causes of forest fires, moorland bush fires
- Look at places where volcanoes have been
- Fire and pollution

Science

- Experiments using fire *AT1, AT3*
- Candles need air *AT3*
- Produce carbon soot *AT3*
- Cooking changes things *AT3*
- Fire strengthens things – metal *AT3*
- Sun can burn things – magnifying glass *AT4*
- Smoke detectors *AT4*
- Flammable and flame retardant materials *AT3*

Religious Education

- Fire – symbol of strength
- Symbol of Holy Spirit
- Links with Hallowe'en, November 5th, Diwali
- Candles in places of worship

History

- Cavemen and fire
- King Alfred burning the cakes
- Light before electricity
- Rush-lights/candles/oil lamps
- History of fire-engines – stately homes often have their own
- Fire of London – children as chimney sweeps
- Beacons

1 Fire is hot.
2 Fire is dangerous.
3 Fire burns things and can change them permanently.

4 Fire can help us with heat, light and energy.
5 Fire needs air to burn.

● Try to arrange a visit to your local fire station, or if that is not possible try to arrange a visit to your school by the local fire-brigade. Most fire stations are willing to send a fire-engine and a crew to give demonstrations. They will also supply a good range of fire prevention posters. Perhaps your local area has a mascot. In the north-west of England, and some other areas, the fire-brigade mascot is Wellephant, a huge red elephant dressed as a fireman. Wellephant will visit schools and talk to the children about safety and fire prevention.

● Fireman Sam is a popular children's character and there are videos and books available which put across the message of safety in a way that the children can understand. Ask the children to bring in toy fire-engines, and even the Ghostbusters' fire-station can be used. If one of the children has a parent who is a fire-fighter, they may be able to lend you some pieces of equipment, or come in and talk about their job.

● Talk about volcanoes and watch David Attenborough's, *Living Planet* series. Talk about energy from the sun and the fact that it is a ball of fire. Look at fossil fuels such as coal, gas and oil, and talk about the ways in which we get energy and heat from these.

● Make a collection of photographs and pictures of the sun and sunsets. Display these with a variety of candles and oil lamps.

● Try to collect a set of suitable books that the children can refer to during the topic, such as books which deal with fire, fuels, volcanoes, geysers and thermal springs.

CM1 –3

Give the children a chance to help with mounting the display, and also let them look through the topic books. Watch the videos together and talk with the children about what they have seen. Discuss any visits you may have had from people, and talk about how the children feel about the dangers of fire and the terrible injuries even a small fire can cause to a human being.

Video a real fire

If any parent has a camcorder, they may like to video a real fire, either a bonfire in the garden, or a coal fire in the hearth. This could be the stimulus for imaginative writing and poetry. Try to include pictures of the fire being lit and the fire at its height. As it dies down, look at the smouldering embers and ashes. As you play the video, try to get the children to talk about what the flames remind them of, and to listen carefully to the noises at the different stages of the fire. Have a big sheet of paper to jot down ideas, or use the vocabulary sheet. Remember to look at, and talk about, the smoke and the sparks as well as the flames.

Reportive writing

The children can write about their visit to a fire station, or of the visit of the fire-engine to school. Writing may be about any scientific activities or Technology, or indeed any other area of the curriculum.

Imaginative writing

Read stories about fire-breathing dragons, or the legend of the phoenix. Discuss with the children what it would be like to have such a creature as a pet, or indeed to have to try to fight such a thing. The children can try to imagine what life would be like as a fire-fighter. Try to find out about the people who have had to try to extinguish fires on an oil-rig, and write an adventure story. The television series *Thunderbirds* is an excellent source of inspiration for such a story, as the children really identify with the crew of International Rescue. For further ideas, see *Blueprints Writing* for such titles as: Bonfire night, When I grow up, Special machine, My dragon, and A newspaper.

Talk about the joys of sitting by a warm cosy fire on a cold damp night, or sitting round a camp fire, roasting potatoes. Contrast this with the feelings that might be experienced if the children were trapped inside a blazing building with no means of escape.

Make warning posters about the dangers of fire. Not just in the home, but in open spaces too. Try to create a list of safety rules for school and home by discussing with the children the sorts of things that can cause fires. Talk about the Firework Code on Bonfire night.

Try to find poems about fire and songs like, 'London's burning', to give the children a few ideas about what images fire has conjured up in other people's imagination. Look for: 'The burning' by Ted

Walker; 'Autumn fires' by Robert Louis Stevenson; 'Bonfire' by Ebele Modu; 'Safe' by James Walker; 'The dreadful story of Harriet and the matches' by Hoffman; 'James, the hero of the fire' from *A golden treasury* edited by James Reeves.

Copymasters

Copymaster 1 (Cover sheet) can be used as a cover for the topic folder with the title written in the space in the middle. It can also be used for imaginative writing, or for a poem or piece of blank verse. The children can write about their general impressions of fire, or the sheet can be enlarged as a class vocabulary sheet, or used at A4 size as the child's personal vocabulary sheet.

Use **Copymaster 2** (Fire match) to encourage the children to use nouns, adjectives and adverbs together when describing fire. An example of this might be, 'dancing flames'. The children look at the group of words at the top and try to link them with one of the words at the bottom. This can be done as a group exercise, as a discussion, or for the more able children to attempt on their own.

Use **Copymaster 3** (Dangers from fire) for the children to identify the most common causes of fire. This will help them in the discussion about fire-safety rules, and they can then colour in the pictures. To help to remind them of any potential dangers, they can cut the pictures out and stick them in appropriate places around school, class or home.

MATHEMATICS

Make a sundial

On a sunny day drive a stake into the ground and, on the hour, mark where the shadow lies by placing a stone. Do this at each consecutive hour throughout the whole school day, and at the end of the day you will have an efficient sundial.

Sundial

Make a candle clock

This activity takes a long time, and care must be taken to ensure complete safety. You will need two candles the same size. Make sure they are well secured and there is no danger of them falling over, and ensure they are out of reach to prevent them being knocked over or caught. Place the two candles side by side and light one of them. After one hour, mark the level of the lit candle on the unlit one. Adult supervision is needed at all times when dealing with naked flame, and the children should wear gloves to avoid drips of molten wax. Repeat this process each hour until the first candle has burned down, and you will then have a candle clock marked in hours.

Candle clock

Collecting information for graphs

Information can be collected for simple picture graphs by carrying out a survey among the children to discover what type of fire, or heating, they have at home. Types of fire can include coal, gas, electric, wood-burning stove, other. 'Other' may include oil-filled radiator, calor gas® heater, and storage heater. Another survey can be carried out to discover what type of central heating they have.

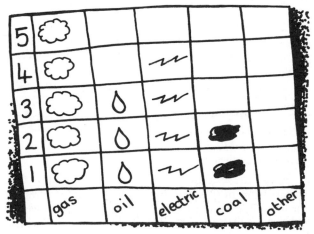

Types of fire in the home

83

Carry out a survey of those families which have a smoke detector and emphasise the need to check that it works properly and that the batteries are still good.

Mention also that most people die of smoke inhalation rather than burns.

Fire needs air

For this experiment, you will need two candles and a large glass jar. As with all experiments and demonstrations involving fire, you must at all times have the safety of the children uppermost in your mind, and take suitable precautions.

Light the candles and watch them burn. Now place the glass jar over one of the candles. After a short while the flame will flicker and die. Ask the children why they think that happened. Then ask whether they think the other candle will go out if you place the jar over that one. Discuss their observations and talk about fire and smoke. Is it the smoke that causes the fire to go out? What happens if you blow on the glowing end of the wick?

Fire changes things

For a dramatic demonstration of this, collect together in a box a variety of different objects made from different materials. Try to include some wood, plastic, metal, leather, paper, wool, nylon, stone, and potatoes in a tin box. Try to have two examples of the materials, one to go into the fire and the other one to compare with afterwards. Make a bonfire in a suitable place away from any other building, and place each of the objects on or into the unlit bonfire. Discuss with the children what they think will happen to each of the objects and try to record this with a simple checklist.

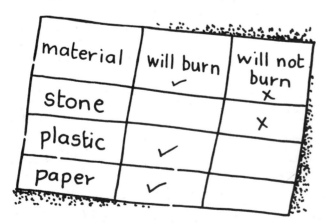

Bonfire checklist

Stand the children well back and light the fire. Observation of this real fire will be a good inspiration for imaginative writing and poetry. Sing some camp-fire songs at the same time, and talk about the way the smoke billows and curls, and how the sparks fly and the flames dance. When the flames die down, look at the glowing embers and ashes, and then leave the fire to go out. Make sure that the fire is completely out and cold before returning to it to look for the remains of the objects that were placed on the fire. There will be no trace of some of the objects, some will be twisted and changed in different ways, and some will hardly have changed at all except for the addition of carbon soot. Make a display of the objects to show how fire has changed them. The potatoes in the tin will be soft enough to eat. Compare the items that went on the fire with the ones that did not go on the fire, and include these in your display.

Heat changes things

Another simple experiment can show that heat changes things, using a calor gas® burner or the school cooker. Extreme care is needed when using heat or fire and this experiment should only be done by an adult. A small group of children can observe and discuss what they think is happening. Put some ice-cubes in a pan and hold them over the heat. The ice will change to water. If we keep heating the water it will eventually boil and change to steam, so we can show that the heat or fire has changed the solid ice-cubes into water, a liquid, then into steam, a gas.

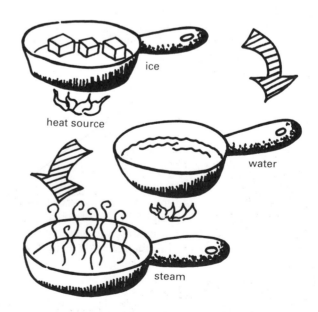

Use **Copymaster 4** (Fire changes things) to record the changes to the materials when they were exposed to the fire. The children can either draw a picture of their object, or if the sample is not too bulky it can be stuck on to the sheet.

Cooking things can change them

We can boil or fry an egg, and compare it with a raw egg. We can mix the ingredients for a cake, and leave a little of the mixture in a small bowl while placing the rest of the mixture in a cake tin and baking it in a hot oven. When the cake is done, and it has cooled down sufficiently, let the children taste the mixture and compare it with the baked cake. You can also show that you need to give just the right amount of heat and for the correct amount of time, otherwise the cake too gets burned and it is not good to eat. A quicker demonstration of this would be to prepare toast. Show them a slice of toast which is underdone, a golden brown piece and a burned blackened piece.

Fire and the sun

For this experiment you will need a day when there is strong sunlight, and a good magnifying glass. As before, stress the importance of safety and care. Concentrate the sun's rays through the magnifying glass on to a piece of paper which is affixed with Sellotape® to the bottom of a metal baking tray. Let the children observe what happens and then let them try to explain, in their own way, the reason why.

Protective clothing and materials

Fire-fighters need to be protected when fighting fires,

so their clothes are made of a special material which does not catch fire easily. Talk about flame retardent materials and look for labels on clothes and soft furnishings. Discuss why we need these materials in our homes. Talk about the materials used in house construction and identify those which are likely to burn and those which are less likely to burn, based upon the children's observations in the earlier activities.

TECHNOLOGY

Design fire-fighting equipment

Let the children look at the different pieces of fire-fighting equipment, and see if they can come up with any ideas for improving it. Look at the breathing apparatus, fire-engines, protective clothing, and the tools for gaining access to buildings. They can try to design their own fire-engine, or a suit of protective clothing for the fireman of the future. Give them an opportunity to build a fire-escape from a doll's-house, using Lego® or Duplo®. Using any suitable construction toy, let them try to build a vehicle to carry a container

of water. A simple fire-engine can be made by building a basic chassis from Lego®, with axles and wheels. A washing-up liquid bottle can be fastened to the top of the vehicle, and a length of clear plastic tubing for the hose can be attached to the nozzle. The water can be squirted by squeezing the bottle. Of course the children will also have their own ideas.

In the past, water had to be carried by hand to put fires out, and the water usually came from a well. See *Blueprints Topics 5–8* (p. 111), for details of how to build a simple mechanism for lifting gear for a well.

plastic bottle

Simple fire-engine

85

Paintings of fire and sunsets

Using the warm colours of red, orange, yellow, pink and purple, ask the children to paint fiery pictures of flames or bonfires. The same colours can be used for a sunset picture, and as an inspiration the works of the artist Turner are ideal. Photographs from calendars and postcards often depict beautiful sunsets, and these too are a good source of inspiration. Wax crayon pictures of fireworks and explosions can be created by starting from a chosen point, and drawing lines of colour radiating from that point. A wash of black watercolour paint over the top of the design gives a good effect. The sheets are then mounted on activity paper, and displayed together for best effect.

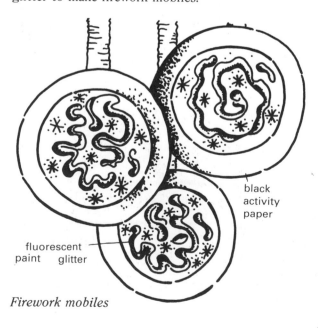

Fireworks display

Dribbling fluorescent paint on to black activity paper in swirls and spirals creates interesting patterns, and these can be highlighted by the addition of a little glitter to make firework mobiles.

Firework mobiles

Dribbling melted coloured wax on to activity paper produces a good textured surface. As before, remember the safety aspects and ensure an adult is present to supervise. Take care when mounting this work as the wax is very brittle and breaks easily.

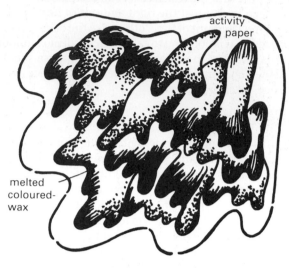

Wax transfer pictures

Children draw and colour a design using thick wax crayons for maximum coverage. This can then be transferred on to another sheet of paper to create a good textured print by placing the wax design face downward on the second sheet, and pressing them with a hot iron. The two sheets should be displayed side by side to show the contrast.

Wax transfer pictures

Simple batik

The children draw a design in pencil on a piece of white cloth and then, with adult supervision, go over the design with a brush dipped in melted wax. Leave the wax to harden and then crumple up the cloth to crack the wax. The material can then be soaked in cold-water dye, or painted with different coloured water-based inks or felt tip pens. Place the material between two sheets of brown paper and press with a hot iron to remove the wax.

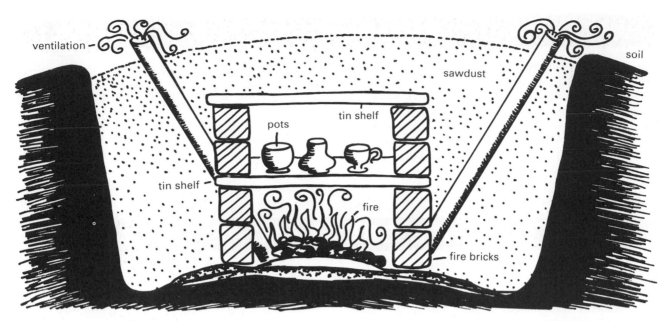

Build a sawdust kiln.

Firing clay

Let the children make models with clay which can then be fired in a kiln. There is a range of new modelling materials which can be baked in a regular oven. The children can then observe the changes brought about by fire.

A sawdust kiln can be built in the school grounds by digging a small pit and lining it with fire bricks. Place a tin lid on top of the bricks to form a shelf and place the clay pots on this. Put more rows of fire bricks around the pots and place another shelf on top. Fill the pit with sawdust. Leave some holes for ventilation so that the fire will burn and the smoke can escape, and light the fire. This will burn very slowly and it can be left for a few days. The curls of smoke will signify that the fire is burning, and a careful check will need to be made to monitor progress. After a suitable period of time, make a hole in the top of the sawdust and inspect one of the pots. If it is not fired sufficiently, put it back and relight the kiln. Do this until the pots are fired.

Charcoal drawings

The children can draw from direct observation using charcoal sticks. This can be very messy at first, but with practice and a little patience they will get used to handling the medium, and any smudges can be cleaned up at the end with a pencil eraser. The finished picture can then be sprayed with an aerosol fixative.

Volcano pictures

Use paper, dribbled wax and tissue-paper. Start off by painting a picture of a mountain, then drip coloured wax around the edge of the crater to represent molten lava. Cut out tissue flames and stick these in place, and add a sprinkling of glitter to represent the sparks and flames.

Volcano picture

Listen to the way in which composers have interpreted fire in their music, for example: the *Royal fireworks music* (Handel); *Ritual fire dance* (De Falla); *Firebird suite* (Stravinsky). Try to find popular songs such as: 'London's burning'; 'Fire down below', a sea-shanty; 'This little light of mine'; 'Fire and flame' by Jack Bainbridge; 'Candle in the wind' by Elton John; 'Fire – I'll teach you to burn'.

Simple accompaniment

Use **Copymaster 5** (Fire songs) for the children to pick out on chime bars or glockenspiel. A simple ostinati is shown above the line which can accompany the played tune or singing.

DANCE, DRAMA AND PE

DANCE

In movement and dance lessons, talk about the movement of the fire: leaping flames, dancing sparks, swirling smoke. Try to develop a simple sequence of movements based upon a fire flickering into life, growing and roaring into action with flames leaping and twisting up into the air, then slowing down and dying to smouldering embers and ashes. Let the children work individually at first, to create their own movement vocabulary. Then they can work together in small groups to represent bigger fires, and finally all work together as a huge bonfire. Use some non-tuned percussion to accompany the final stages or, if you prefer, some stirring orchestral music with a softer finale to represent the fire dying. This idea can be developed further by asking the children to represent objects being consumed by the flames. This can be based upon their own experiences of having watched the bonfire and the effects on the objects placed in it (see p. 84). They could pretend to be wax melting or paper curling as it burns.

DRAMA

In the role-play centre, the children can try to improvise situations they have seen in the videos of Fireman Sam, or pretend to be actual firemen and rescue people from blazing buildings. Turn the home corner into a fire station complete with telephones and two-way radio. Try to make some outfits and get some of the plastic fireman's hats available from toy warehouses. Cardboard axes and pretend breathing apparatus, or some real borrowed equipment, will help create the right atmosphere.

RELIGIOUS EDUCATION

Fire as symbol

Look at fire as a symbol of strength. Fire is used to strengthen steel. It is also the symbol of the Holy Spirit in Christian faith, and was used to give confidence and inner strength to the apostles after Christ's death. Look at the significance of fire and flame in other religions. Talk about Divali, Hallowe'en, and November 5th. Find out how fire is used in religious ceremonies and the significance of candles. Look at the ancient customs of the Druids, when they lit bonfires to welcome the sun back after the dark days of winter. Discuss midsummer bonfires and fire festivals, such as 'Up Helly Aa' in the Shetland Isles, and read the story of Shadrach, Meshach and Abednego.

HISTORY

Early fires and lamps

Try to find out about the first fires, maybe they were started by lightning striking, and talk about the ways in which early man discovered how to make fire. Try to get some flints and strike them together to make sparks, or try rubbing twigs together to see if they get hot. Link this with science and discuss friction. Talk about the usefulness of fire to early man and discuss what life would have been like without all the comforts we take for granted. Talk about how fire was used to keep wild animals away from caves, and how food first began to be cooked by roasting it on a fire.

Take the children to a castle where the huge kitchens can be seen and, if possible, show them the massive roasting spits where whole cows would be roasted. Think about how fire was also used for lighting. Make a rush-light to show the children how well they gave light, and try and create a display of different kinds of lamps from reproduction Roman lamps and the type used by Aladin, to the very ornate Victorian oil lamps. Include also a selection of different candlesticks and, if possible, tinder-boxes and tallow-candles. Pictures will do if you cannot get the real thing. Allow the children to handle the smaller artefacts. Try to have modern equivalents of all the objects so that the children can compare them, and do, at all times, stress the dangers of playing with fire.

Fire as messenger

Talk about fire as a messenger. There may be a beacon hill near to where you live and you can explain that when there were no telephones to aid communication, one of the quickest ways of sending news was to light beacons. They were usually used to warn of danger of attack, or to tell of the birth of a royal baby. A fire would be lit on the top of the highest hill in the neighbourhood, and this would be seen from a great distance, by people living in the next county. They would then light their beacon and so pass the message on.

Try to find out about the children who had to work as chimney-sweeps in Victorian London and the

dangers they had to face. Also find out about the young children who had to work down the mines. Ask the children in your class whether they would like to have to do such a thing.

Early fire-engines

Look at fire-engines and see how they have developed. Many country houses had their own fire-engine and fire-brigade. If you do visit a large estate to look at the kitchens, keep a look out for the estate fire-engine, or ask what was the usual thing to happen in the event of a fire.

Use **Copymaster 6** (Fire-engines) to make a stand-up model of an old fire-engine and another of a modern fire-fighter. This can be used to create a diorama of a team of fire-fighters tackling a blazing building. The children can draw their own houses and colour them for the background. Then stick the fire-engine on to a piece of stiff card and colour it and cut it out. By glueing a matchbox to the back, it will be free-standing and can be positioned as required.

Read stories about the Great Fire of London, the story of how King Alfred burned the cakes, and any others which have a link with fire.

GEOGRAPHY

Volcanoes

Look at volcanoes by watching relevant episodes of *The Living Planet* video by David Attenborough. Collect together as many books as possible on the subject, especially those which have spectacular pictures and photographs. Look also for information about geysers and thermal springs. Look at a world map and try to find out where some of the most famous of these are situated. Ask the children if they notice anything about their location. Discuss recent eruptions of volcanoes in the Philippines, and of Mount St Helens in America, and Mount Etna in Italy.

Use **Copymaster 7** (Volcano) to talk about what happens inside a volcano. The cloze procedure at the bottom of the sheet will help the children to focus on the important points. Talk about the danger to wildlife and the environment. Discuss the relationship between forest fires, bush fires and moorland fires, and their relationship with dry windy weather.

Fire in the local environment

Look at the local area. Are there any coal-mines or open-cast mining? Do these have a bad effect on the local environment? Is there an oil refinery nearby? Discuss pollution from there, and consider whether it is air pollution or the danger of leakage into rivers which could have an effect on wildlife. Talk about pollution from the factories which use fire to create their products, and talk about the dangerous fumes that can be given off when certain materials are burned such as rubber, plastics and foam.

Make a plan of your school and mark on it all the fire-exits and the sites of the fire-extinguishers and the alarms. Go out into the local area and look for the fire-hydrants and the water-mains. As part of fire precautions, make sure that all the children know how to summon the emergency services and do stress that they should only call them in an emergency so that everyone who needs help has the chance to receive it.

Fire 1

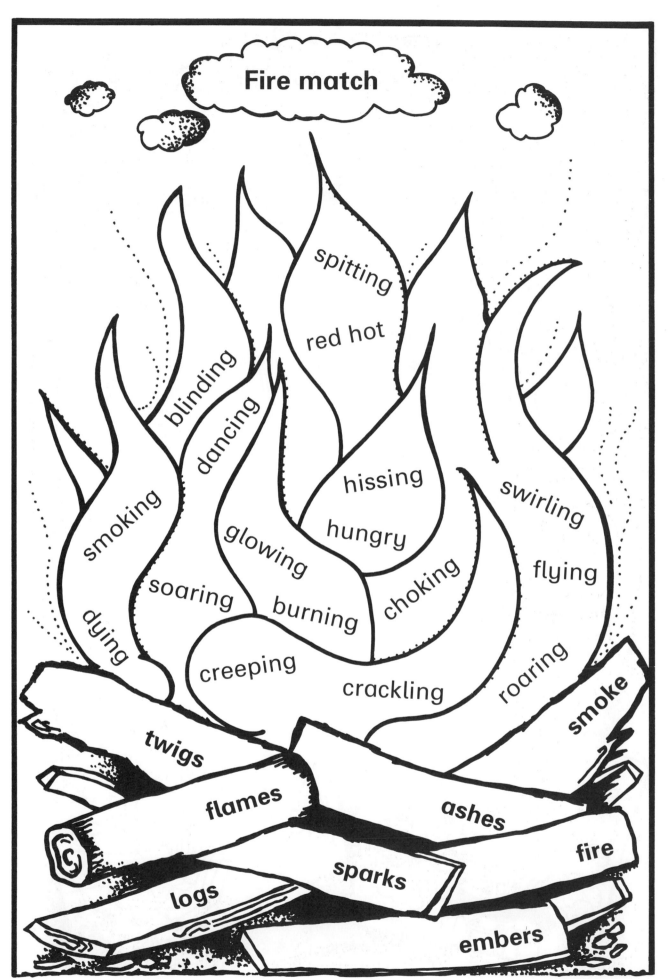

Fire 2

Dangers from fire

unguarded fires and heaters

children playing with matches

clothing left to dry on fireguard

too many plugs in socket

cards on a fireplace

chip-pan catching fire

putting hot ashes in bins

old people smoking in bed

Fire changes things

Object	What happened
candle + 🔥 =	
plastic spoon + 🔥 =	
wood + 🔥 =	
stone + 🔥 =	
butter + 🔥 =	
paper + 🔥 =	
metal spoon + 🔥 =	
+ 🔥 =	

Fire songs

Twinkle twinkle little star

London's burning

Fire down below

Fire-engines

Volcano

hot ash

lava flow

molten rock

Complete the sentences below by filling in the missing words.

In the centre of the earth is _____.

The top of a volcano is called the _____.

Melted rock from a volcano is called _____.

Volcanoes also produce showers of hot _____.

| ash | crater | molten rock | lava |

MY BODY

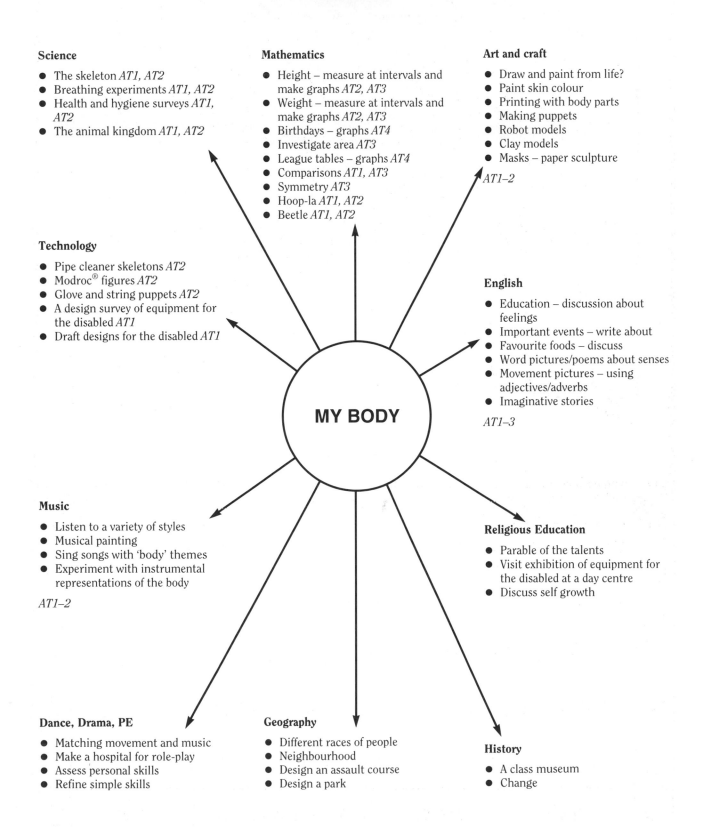

Science

- The skeleton *AT1, AT2*
- Breathing experiments *AT1, AT2*
- Health and hygiene surveys *AT1, AT2*
- The animal kingdom *AT1, AT2*

Technology

- Pipe cleaner skeletons *AT2*
- Modroc® figures *AT2*
- Glove and string puppets *AT2*
- A design survey of equipment for the disabled *AT1*
- Draft designs for the disabled *AT1*

Mathematics

- Height – measure at intervals and make graphs *AT2, AT3*
- Weight – measure at intervals and make graphs *AT2, AT3*
- Birthdays – graphs *AT4*
- Investigate area *AT3*
- League tables – graphs *AT4*
- Comparisons *AT1, AT3*
- Symmetry *AT3*
- Hoop-la *AT1, AT2*
- Beetle *AT1, AT2*

Art and craft

- Draw and paint from life?
- Paint skin colour
- Printing with body parts
- Making puppets
- Robot models
- Clay models
- Masks – paper sculpture

AT1–2

English

- Education – discussion about feelings
- Important events – write about
- Favourite foods – discuss
- Word pictures/poems about senses
- Movement pictures – using adjectives/adverbs
- Imaginative stories

AT1–3

Music

- Listen to a variety of styles
- Musical painting
- Sing songs with 'body' themes
- Experiment with instrumental representations of the body

AT1–2

Religious Education

- Parable of the talents
- Visit exhibition of equipment for the disabled at a day centre
- Discuss self growth

Dance, Drama, PE

- Matching movement and music
- Make a hospital for role-play
- Assess personal skills
- Refine simple skills

Geography

- Different races of people
- Neighbourhood
- Design an assault course
- Design a park

History

- A class museum
- Change

BASIC CONCEPTS

1 All people belong to the human race.

2 Humans are mammals and part of the animal kingdom.

3 Each part of our body has a different structure and function.

4 The brain and our emotions control the actions of our bodies.

5 In order to function and grow well, the body needs food, water, shelter and exercise plus love and companionship.

6 Each human being is special and unique and has their own needs and desires.

7 Sometimes illness, disability, abuse or neglect can affect the body's function.

STARTING POINTS

● Children can watch a short video of an athletics meeting, swimming event, gymnastics display, or any sporting or leisure activity. (See below in the PE section for a copymaster.)

● Collect magazine photographs of faces, and the children's own photographs of themselves showing different emotions such as anger, surprise, sadness, pleasure.

● Collect pictures of people engaged in a variety of skills, both intellectual and physical, such as horse-riding, reading, painting, cooking or cycling. You can then make these into a montage of human skills, and get the children to make a personal catalogue of their own skills.

● Make a collection of protective clothes and equipment and display them as a starting point for discussion.

● There are many ingenious inventions to help the disabled and children will find such a collection fascinating. There are hearing-aids and cup fillers, flashing lights and wheelchairs, subtitles and guide dogs.

ENGLISH

CM1 –2

Self-portrait

Using the picture collection of faces, discuss emotions with the children and ask them to think about their feelings and what events cause different emotional reactions. What makes you feel really happy, sad, angry? Look at the pictures and try to decide what emotions are shown on the faces. Ask the children to draw a large self-portrait showing a chosen emotion, and to add a speech bubble in which they can write about how the emotion makes them feel.

Personal stories and diaries

Get the children to write stories about important events in their lives as part of a personal history.

Make a diary for the children to take home or use in

school. Try using unusual shapes or sizes to add even more interest to the exercise.

Shaped books

Lists of preferences

Discuss personal preferences for food and encourage the children to give reasons for their answers. They could work in groups for discussions to exchange ideas. Make lists of personal preferences for things like TV programmes, books, sports, and so on. Try to get them to put these in order of preference too. Draw your own copymaster or get the children to design one on which to write such lists. One example is illustrated below.

Word pictures

Write simple poetry or word pictures, using the senses as a starting point. Bring in a collection of objects with different smells, such as perfume, baby talc, soap, vinegar, tomato sauce, pepper, butter, bread, and so on. Encourage the children to say what impression comes into their minds, whether the smell is pleasant, nasty, exciting, delicious, makes them think of summer or autumn, or whatever. Ask them to write down the single ideas that come into their minds as a word picture, one impression on each line. For example: It's sharp; It tickles; It bites your nose; It's juicy; It's delicious; It's vinegar on chips.

Movement pictures

Write movement pictures taking a dance or PE lesson as the starting point and discuss the movements that the children have made, widening their descriptive vocabulary by suggesting adverbs and adjectives. Try the movements, discuss feelings about them, and do them again so that the children are thinking about their impressions as they move. Try writing the word pictures in a shape that suggests the movement.

Write imaginative stories

Get the children to pretend they have super-powers and discuss what these might be. Would they have super-vision or hearing, or would they have the power of flight or super-strength? Maybe they would opt for a super-brain to out-wit all adversaries.

Alternatively, try to get them to imagine what it would be like to lose one of their senses, or the movement in one part of their body. To help them you may know someone who is disabled who would be willing to talk to children.

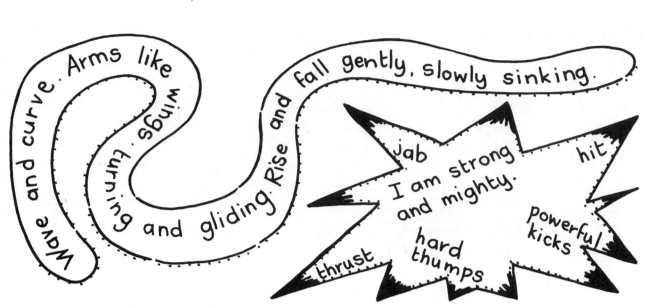

Movement pictures

Copymaster 1 (Cover sheet) is a decorative sheet showing bodies engaged in different activities. It can be used for the imaginative writing, reportive writing on the visit of a disabled person, poetry, or as a cover for the topic book.

Copymaster 2 (Parts of the body) is a picture of a body which needs labelling. It is an exercise in matching and reading. Ask the children to use the formula, 'Look, cover, write', as they fill in the labels.

MATHEMATICS

Height

Start off by measuring the children's height, preferably at the beginning of the year so that you can remeasure at intervals to check progress.

Copymaster 3 (Height) is a height graph. This can be enlarged to A3 size to use for wall display, or kept at A4 for individuals to use. To enlarge the horizontal axis, cover the vertical axis and photocopy this. Stick together as many sheets as are needed to fit on the whole class. Alternatively, each table or group could keep their own height chart, or individuals could keep a monthly record of their growth by labelling the horizontal axis as months instead of children's names. Colour the vertical columns in different colours for each child, or in two alternating colours for individual records.

An actual height graph is useful visually and conceptually. For this use the manufactured metre-long centimetre paper strips. The children can be measured on a wall ruler and take a metre strip plus the required number of extra centimetres to make their height. Have these coloured in individual patterns and stick on to a large sheet of paper as a wall display, but do put the bottom of the sheet at floor level so that the children can compare the height at eye level. They can add extra centimetres to their column as they grow.

Weight

Record weight in the same way, using bar graphs. It may be useful to make comparisons of height and weight for individuals to see if the heaviest children are also the tallest. It is a good idea to make the point that as children are constantly growing, many who seem over heavy at one stage may simply be going through a growth spurt.

Time and the body

Make a birthday chart, but instead of a bar graph record the information on a pie chart as shown opposite. See if there are any observations to be made regarding the age of the children and their size. Are the children with the September birthdays bigger than those with August birthdays? You can make the point that individuals often inherit their family body size as well as shape. Do the tall children come from tall families?

Investigate area

Make a graph of shoe size then follow this up by drawing round the sole of the shoe on centimetre squared paper, and then counting the number of squares to get an idea of area. If this is done as accurately as possible, the children should be able to see that the larger size shoes have the larger area, and vice versa. You can try to work out the area of feet and hands too.

League tables

To help make the point that individuals differ in their physical, intellectual and social accomplishments,

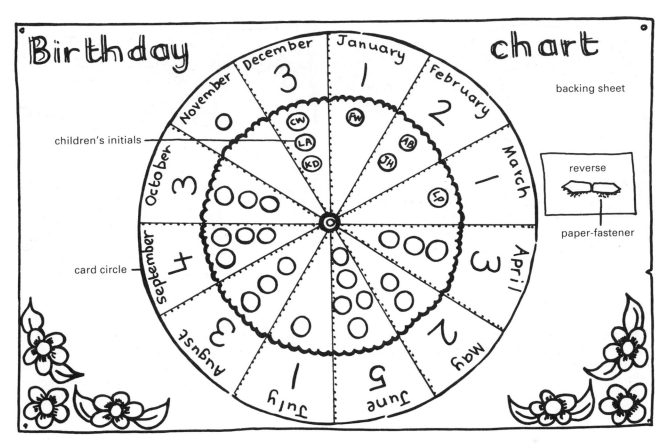

Birthday chart

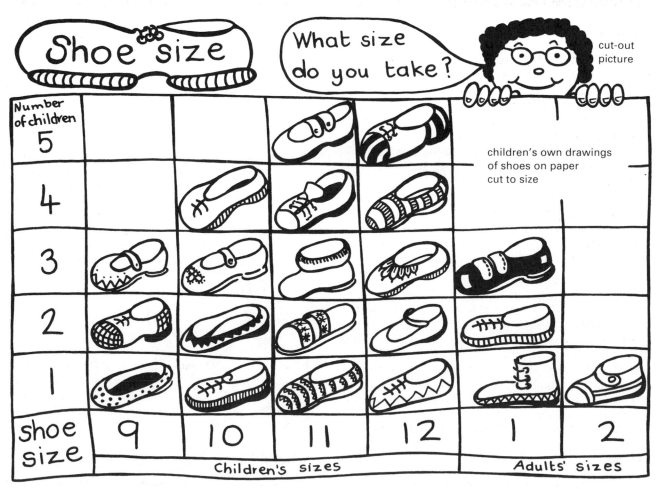

Shoe size

keep a star chart or a points chart for achievements. These build up over a period of time into a graphic record, and individuals will be able to see their own progress in different areas. You can occasionally involve the class in decisions of award, but do be careful to find areas of success for each pupil, preferably in each category so that a pupil doesn't see himself as a failure in one area.

More comparisons

Using standard and non-standard measurements, compare sizes of different parts of the body. Measure the length of arms, legs, span, cubit, strides, paces, jumps or throws. With jumps you can measure the length or the height, but the latter is more difficult to assess and will need much discussion as to how the test can be made fair.

Symmetry

As part of some work on symmetry, look at how the body can be made to look symmetrical. Try different body positions in PE, both symmetrical and asymmetrical. Let the children work individually or with a partner to create a symmetrical shape. Back in the classroom, ask them to draw a body in a symmetrical position. Use squared paper to help accuracy. They can also attempt to draw some of the positions they attempted in PE.

Hoop-la

Make a hoop-la board by drawing a large figure with arms and legs outstretched (30 cm by 40 cm is a good size for this). Colour it and paste it on to a piece of stiff card. Stick self-adhesive plastic hooks on each of the

main body parts as shown. Write a number alongside each hook which is the score for making a hoop-la. Contestants can add up their score as they play. The children can make up their own rules, for example four throws for each player and the highest score wins. Rubber washers seem the best weight for hoops.

Beetle

Another game using an accumulation of points and adding parts to a whole is beetle. Instead of drawing a beetle, let the children draw a human body and use the same rules as for beetle.

SCIENCE

CM4

The skeleton

Borrow a full-size skeleton from a Teachers' Centre or a local secondary school, and explore it with the children. Observe the position of the joints and how they articulate. Move the limbs of the skeleton and get the children to mirror the movements with their own bodies.

Draw the skeleton from 'life', encouraging the children to observe very carefully the size, shape and position of the bones. Use balloons to show the positions of the major organs which the skeleton protects, like the lungs, heart and brain.

Use **Copymaster 4** (Skeleton) which is a pieced drawing of a skeleton. The children can colour it in and then cut round the outlines. The skeleton can then be joined together with paper-clips and mounted on a wall, each one in a different position. If desired, it can be made into a puppet by taping sticks or paper rolls into position as shown.

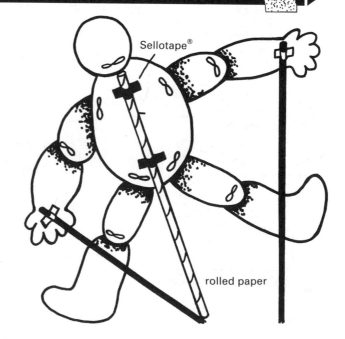

Sellotape®

rolled paper

Breathing

Set up some simple experiments to show that breathing, the heart rate and exercise are all connected. Show the children how to feel the heart-beat or pulse, and if possible use a stethoscope to listen to the heart and lungs working. To show how exercise affects these rates, record the heart and breathing rates of several children when they are at rest and then after violent exercise such as running round the playground twice. Record the different heart and breathing rates by counting the number of breaths per minute and the number of heart-beats per minute both before and after the exercise. The rates after exercise will be much higher. The lungs take in air, the oxygen is passed into the blood and the blood is pumped to the muscles in a rate according to need. So, when the body moves more it needs more energy and the breathing and heart rates increase.

Record this on simple linear charts.

Health and hygiene surveys

Collect advertising and information material about good health and hygiene from commercial and medical sources. Get the children to help make a display for the classroom. As a result of this many questions should arise which are of interest to the children. You can then help them to find the answers by conducting surveys. They need to know how to collect information, identify differences, collate information, record findings and then to interpret this information. They will need guidance on collection of material, construction of questionnaires, design of lists and charts, and how to approach people.

Surveys arising from their own questions could include: Bedtimes and getting up times in the class; Number of hours sleep each night; Hobby activities which give exercise; Number of times teeth cleaned in a day; Types of food eaten; Number of children involved in a road accident; Number of children who know the Green Cross Code. (Taken from *Blueprints Science Key Stage One*, Attainment Target 2, Life and living processes. See this section also for work on reproduction.)

The animal kingdom

Humans are mammals and as such have specialised bodies adapted to a certain lifestyle. It is useful to look

into this with the children to learn about the structure and function of the body and to develop a wider view of the world's life forms. All mammals have a skeleton, teeth adapted for eating different foods, and hair or fur. They are warm-blooded, they bear live young, and the females give milk to the young.

Outline the structure of the animal kingdom using toy animals and pictures and make this into a hands-on display so that the children can sort the animals themselves.

Bearing in mind DES and LEA regulations about animals in school, and the safety of the animals, try to bring in some examples of mammals and their young and observe the body structure and the likeness of parents and young. A parent may be willing to bring in a baby so that the children can compare their own bodies with that of the baby.

TECHNOLOGY

Pipe cleaner skeletons

Using a model skeleton or a picture of the skeleton as an example, try modelling with pipe cleaners. Start off with a single pipe cleaner as the backbone and join others on to it by twisting the ends tightly round the main line. Discuss how to join the pipe cleaners before you start the job.

Twisted pipe cleaners sometimes work loose if handled, so you may need to discuss remedies for this technical difficulty.

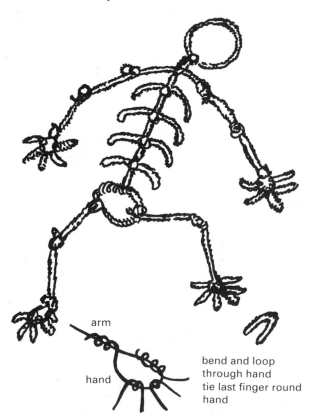

arm

hand

bend and loop through hand
tie last finger round hand

Pipe cleaner skeletons

Modroc® figures

To make figures covered in Modroc® you will need to design a skeleton and it will need to be fixed securely to a stable base. You also need to decide what position you want the figure to hold, as this will affect the whole structure, for example you may need a support to hold up an outstretched leg.

Do this as a group activity and discuss the design details, including the proportions of the body, and experiment with the children. For the skeleton try metal coat-hangers, pipe cleaners, twigs, dowelling, rolled newspaper, kitchen roll tubes, small boxes and anything else that can be joined in lengths. You will also need to consider what to use for the base. Try wood, stone, concrete, Plasticine® and other heavy substances that can be found or made into a wide base. Fixing the skeleton to the base will also be an important design task.

For example, wire can push into Plasticine® or be set into plaster, and so on.

When the skeleton is fixed, wind and drape the Modroc® over the base figure. The strips of material can be wound round tightly to give a thin outline, or they can be stretched wide and anchored to give a larger shape. Pad out the parts that you want to look rounded with balls of paper, then bandage over this with the Modroc®.

If a smooth finish is required, then wipe over the finished model with a wet hand to smooth off the plaster.

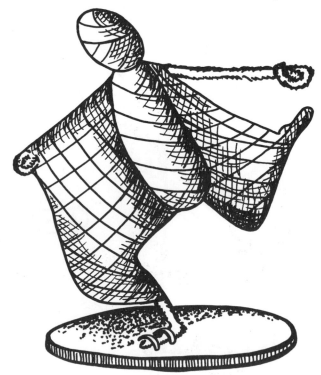

Modroc® figure

Puppets

Try making both glove puppets and string puppets, as they each pose very different design problems.

Glove puppets can be made using a variety of materials for the head. Try cardboard boxes, plastic containers, balloons, papier-mâché over a balloon mould, Modroc® over a ball of paper as the mould, and so on. For the glove use old socks, fabric, paper bags, plastic bags. The trickiest design problem is fixing the head to the glove, so you will need to experiment with different glues, Sellotape®, thin wire, string or wool.

String puppets pose a different problem. For the body, you could consider using card tubes, lolly sticks, plastic straws, balsa wood or heavier wood off-cuts, plastic cups. The problem lies in the joining of the separate limbs to give good articulation. You will need to consider what material to use for the joint and how

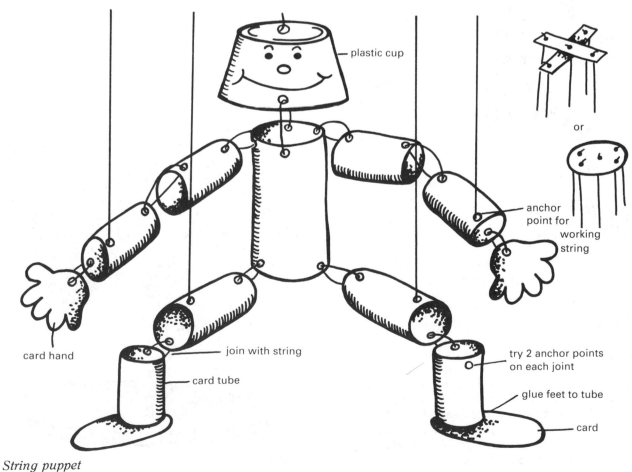

String puppet

105

∿∿ Type of building: school ∿∿			
Feature	hall door	playground	class 5W cloakroom
This is good/ bad	bad- hard to open- narrow	bumpy- no games	not enough room
Suggestion.	Make double doors with hooks to hold them back.	Fill in holes with tarmac. Money from P.T.A.? Children paint on games.	Use old trolley from store for bags. Pull in and out when needed.

to make the holes. For example, you could use fuse wire or thread to joint a lolly stick puppet, but you will need a sharp-pointed tool to make the holes. Do discuss the safety aspects with the children too. Cotton-reels threaded together with string make good, flexible string puppets.

For the working strings you will have to experiment with different lengths and anchor points, but for a first attempt at this type of puppet it is easiest to use just five strings as shown. Use a traditional cross for the puppeteer to hold, or experiment with other designs such as a circle of plastic, card or wood.

A design survey

Use a display of equipment for disabled people as a starting point, and then take a walk round school to see which features of the school building are particularly suitable or unsuitable for people with different types of disability. Look at width of doors and steps for wheel-chair access, positioning and style of furniture, or wall handles in toilets. Use a simple record sheet to make notes as you proceed. This sort of sheet can also be used at home. Try to visit a specialist unit for the disabled to look at their provision.

Draft design for the disabled

Let the children examine some pieces of equipment specially designed for people with varied disabilities, such as cup fillers for the blind, flashing light doorbells for the deaf, helping-hand sticks to help with picking things up off the floor or putting on socks for those with limb disablements.

Use **Copymaster 5** (Draft sheet) for the children to attempt to design a piece of equipment for a particular need. Let them choose a disability, this could be related to someone they know, and then try to design a piece of equipment with this in mind.

ART AND CRAFT

Draw and paint from life

Start off with self-portraits, making a small mirror available for the artists' use. Encourage the children to look at small details such as flecks of different colours in the iris of the eye, or particular shades of colour in the hair. Wax crayons, pencil crayons and felt tips are available in many shades and the children can be encouraged to make their own shades of colour with paint.

Go on to draw portraits of friends. Children can work in pairs asking each other to stand up if they want to observe a detail. Alternatively, you can use one child as a model for a short time so that you can move round the group helping them to observe and draw details of proportion and position. If you put the model in a central position then the group will be able to draw from different viewpoints. You may have to help them

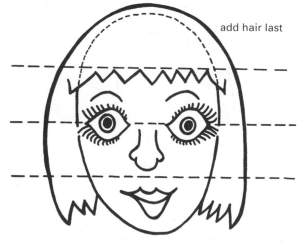
add hair last

Observe proportion and position. Draw an oval and mark it off into quarters to position features.

with this as they often want to draw the front view even if they can't see it. The exercise here is to draw only what can be seen.

Paint skin colour

Have a session of paint mixing where the main object is to mix shades of skin colour. Try to get these as true as possible by matching them to skin types in the class. White skin colour is difficult to make but try starting off with white and adding minute quantities of red and yellow. Add brown to this mix for darker skins. Do this on a small scale with paint-boxes, trying out mixes in small circles on a single sheet of paper.

Printing with body parts

Use hands, fingers, fingerprints, side of fists, feet and forearms to print with paint. Make up figures using a combination of parts. Using white paint on black paper, print a fun skeleton using different parts of the hand.

Decorate puppets

Having designed the puppets in Technology, get down to some serious decoration. For heads with surfaces that need covering, for example a yogurt pot with a printed logo on it, try a variety of paints depending on the surface. Modroc® is very absorbent and will need a large quantity of paint. Plastic surfaces don't take water-based paints well, so mix dry powder paint with PVA glue to the desired colour, and add a little water if the mix is too stiff.

Features can be painted on or cut from coloured paper. Alternatively, items such as dried pulses, buttons, strips of felt or wool can be glued on. Hair can be glued

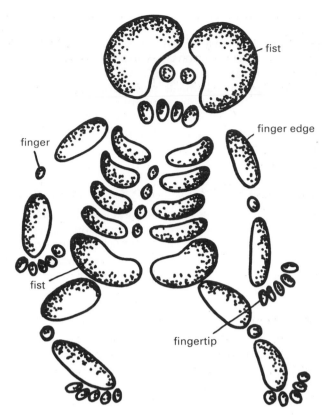

Print a skeleton.

on to the top of heads. Use shredded paper, wool, string, strips of plastic bag or cotton-wool. Provide plenty of choice and try to get as much discussion as possible from exploration of the textures and the technique. Buttons, patches and felt or card hands can be sewn on to the glove of the puppets.

Puppets

107

Robots

Make imaginary robots which have bodies that are suited to their functions. For example, a robot that washes up may need several arms, or one that goes shopping may need wheels, super strider legs and ten arms! Give the children card rolls, boxes, tins, old springs, wood off-cuts or any scrap material. Provide an assortment of glues and tapes to help with construction.

Clay models

If you do not have a kiln, use Newclay. Make simple models of figures in different positions. You can take a fantasy theme and make characters from a story, or you can just make giants and dwarves, or wizards and witches. If this work is done near to Christmas, you could make a clay Nativity scene.

Use simple rolls of clay to construct the figures. Long garments translate well into clay.

Masks

Use simple paper sculpture techniques to make masks from paper plates. Decorate with a variety of scrap materials.

part of broken toy

Robots

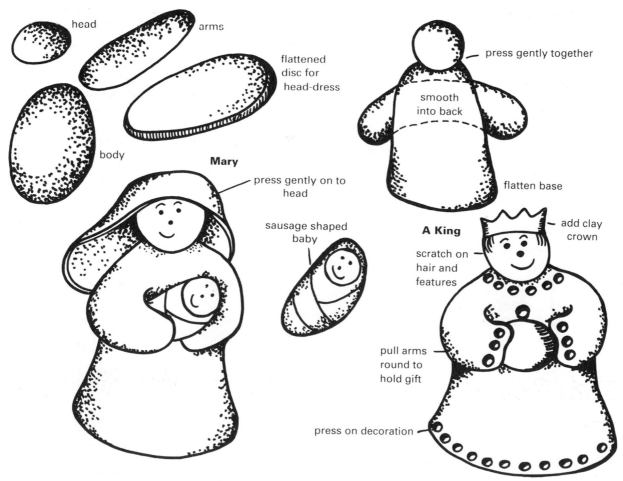

Clay models

108

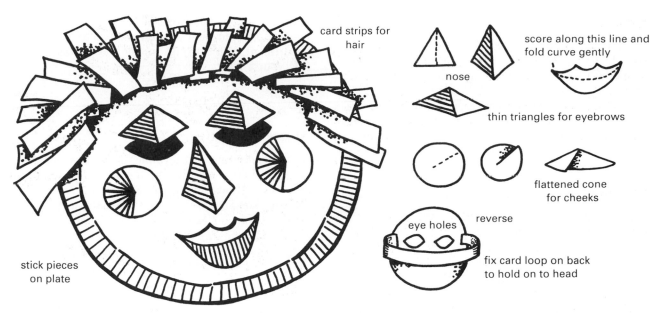

card strips for hair

score along this line and fold curve gently

nose

thin triangles for eyebrows

flattened cone for cheeks

eye holes

reverse

fix card loop on back to hold on to head

stick pieces on plate

Masks

Papier-mâché masks

Use an inflated balloon as a mould and paste on two or three layers of torn-up white paper all over. Let this dry thoroughly and cut the paper balloon·in half length-ways to make two mask bases. Cut eye-holes and decorate with paper sculpture features or paint on features, adding hair later.

MUSIC

Musical appreciation

Listen to a wide variety of different styles and discuss personal preferences.

Musical painting

Prepare paints and paper. Let the children listen to a piece of music and ask them to paint just whatever the music makes them feel like. It may be large sweeping strokes, fast splodges, or thin waving lines. It need not be a picture of anything, just the music translated into a movement on paper. Play the music while they paint and discuss their feelings and impressions.

Try 'Fossils' from the *Carnival of the animals* by Saint-Saëns. This is played on a xylophone and makes most people think of skeletons dancing.

Sing songs

Sing songs to do with the body. The children will probably have lots of suggestions and will enjoy songs that have accompanying actions. The following list suggests a few examples, there are many more.

'Dem bones, dem bones'; 'Heads and shoulders knees and toes'; 'Knees up Mother Brown'; 'If you're happy and you know it'; 'Hands to work and feet to run' (from *Someone's singing Lord*, A. & C. Black); 'One finger, one thumb, one hand, keep moving'.

Experiment with instruments

Use tuned and non-tuned percussion and other instruments if they are available. Try to invent a series of sounds which represent the different movements a body can make. For example, a run on a xylophone could represent a forward roll. Heavy, slow drumbeats could be an old person climbing stairs. Bells shaken could be teeth chattering, and so on.

Ask the children to make up a sound story about what their body does as they get up. For instance, they may open their eyes, yawn, stretch, jump out of bed then fall on the floor and roll about.

DANCE, DRAMA, PE

DANCE

Using the music you have been listening to, this time ask the children to move to it as they feel inspired, simply to express their enjoyment of the music. You may already have started to develop a vocabulary of movement so extend this by discussing with the children which movements come to mind as they listen. Try to identify the music with stretching, curling, twisting, rolling, flowing, gliding movements. Which makes them want to move in short, sharp, spiked movements?

DRAMA

Turn the home corner into a hospital. Parents may be willing to contribute to the equipment by supplying bandages, slings, plastic bowls. You may be able to obtain paper towels and disposable gloves from school or a commercial supplier. Try to find a contact in a hospital to supply you with old X-rays which have been discarded and mount these on a window to provide atmosphere and information about bones. There are many commercially produced toy doctor's kits available which include stethoscopes, syringes, thermometers and other equipment. Include a sharps disposal unit and a gloves disposal unit in the form of cardboard boxes to provide a warning of danger from the real items in the children's play.

Try to arrange a visit to a real hospital or visits from different health workers to the classroom. After they have talked to them, the children will be better able to incorporate the different roles into their play. Do provide the sort of signs and posters they would see in a hospital as part of your language provision.

Give the children situations to act out and develop themselves, and be prepared to observe and intervene if necessary. For example, set up a road accident at one end of the corridor and pick an ambulance crew to come and provide first-aid and removal to the casualty department. You can join in the play by taking on a role yourself.

PE

Assessment

At the beginning of the topic, do an assessment of physical skills to give the children an idea of what they can do at that time. See *Blueprints Topics 5–8*, Copymasters 5 and 6 (physical skills assessment sheets) from the topic on 'Myself'. See also *Blueprints Science Key Stage One Pupils' Copymasters*, Copymasters 9, 12, 13, and 19, for work connected with the body in Science Attainment Target 2.

Refine skills

As part of your PE work, practise some of the simple skills on these sheets such as skipping with a rope and without a rope, jumping from a height, jumping over an obstacle, taking off from two legs and landing on one, balancing on one leg, and so on. For the children who already have these skills, concentrate on refining them and possibly introduce some aspect of record breaking. For example, for those who can balance on

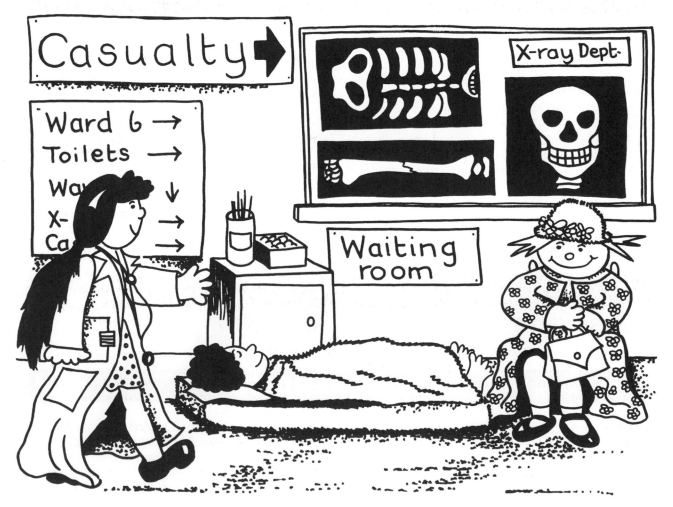

one leg, time how long they can sustain the position. See how many jumps they can do in a row, how fast they can run a certain distance, and so on.

Use **Copymaster 6** (My skills) to record the progress in one skill, or to outline which parts of the body are used in any one skill. The children can draw the activity in the top box and write about which parts of the body were used in the bottom box. They can indicate which parts of the body were used by colouring or ticking the key.

RELIGIOUS EDUCATION

Read the parable of the talents

Discuss how this parable can be applied to the children's lives. Talk about what talents individuals feel they have and what you and the rest of the group think. You may recognise more talents in an individual than they are aware of possessing.

Visits

Visit an exhibition of equipment for disabled people, or try to make contact with a school or a centre for the disabled. It may be possible for you and some children to visit and help on a regular basis. At the very least, your children may be able to make pen-friends or make posters and decorations for the people at the centre. The idea is to try to make friends and see disabled people as people in their own right, and for your children to begin to understand some of the problems of the disabled.

Talk about what it might be like to lose one of the senses or the use of a limb.

Self growth

Discuss self growth with the children. Ask them to bring in some of their toys, books and family artefacts from their own past. This can also form part of the history work. Have a 'show and tell' time where the children can take turns showing one or more items, and explaining about how it was used or why they liked it. Ask them to explain how they feel about these things now. Have they grown and changed? If so, how do they perceive themselves as changed?

HISTORY

Personal history

Make a display of the children's personal history. Ask them to bring in small artefacts and keepsakes from their own past, things which they feel have been important in their growth and ask them to write their own labels explaining, for example, 'This is my teething ring and I chewed it all the time when I was a baby', 'These are my first football boots that I got when I was five years old'.

Change

Ask the children to bring in photographs of themselves at different ages, preferably one for each year of life and compare the children's body shapes and skills at different ages. For example, look at baby pictures and talk about the things babies can do, what age the children started walking or talking, or when they first learnt to ride a bike.

Keep a record of each child's development. Create two copymaster sheets, one headed 'Then', and one headed 'Now'. The idea is for the child to stick a photograph of themselves on to each sheet, one from the past and one from the present. Information about each photograph can then be written underneath.

GEOGRAPHY

Different races

Collect pictures of the different races of humans. There are Caucasian, Negroid, Mongoloid and Aboriginal. You may have children belonging to these races in your class. The point to make is that all of these races are humans and are equal. This can form part of your discussions in RE. Using a globe or a world map, find the places in the world where the different races mostly live. The development of travel has opened up the world so that these races now live together in many Western countries.

Neighbourhood

Look at the neighbourhood around school and do a survey to find out how the children travel to school. Which parts of their body do they use in the journey? Do they travel by car, by bicycle, another form of transport, or do they walk?

Design an assault course and a park

This can be done in plan or pictorial form. It could be for children, adults who need to get fit, older people or disabled people, or toddlers.

My design for a park

Use **Copymaster 7** (My design for a park) for the children to design a park for the needs of the community. A few symbols are already given in the key but the children can think of their own. They need to think where to site the entrance, on the quiet or the busy road. They need to think whether they want play equipment or exercise equipment, and if so what part of the body this will exercise. Do they want trees, ornamental flowers or statues, a quiet place with seats, or maybe a scented garden for the blind. On the energetic side they may want a bike or skateboard track, a football pitch, a jogging track or even a swimming pool. This can be done as a joint exercise for two or three children. The sheet can be enlarged to A3 size for this purpose.

Parts of the body

Put the correct labels on the parts of the body.

chest	ear	hair	leg	elbow	foot
bottom	head	wrist	hand	neck	thigh
arm	ankle	eye	knee	stomach	calf

Height

cm										
150										
140										
130										
120										
110										
100										
90										
80										
70										
60										
50										
40										
30										
20										
10										
0										
Names of children										

My body 3

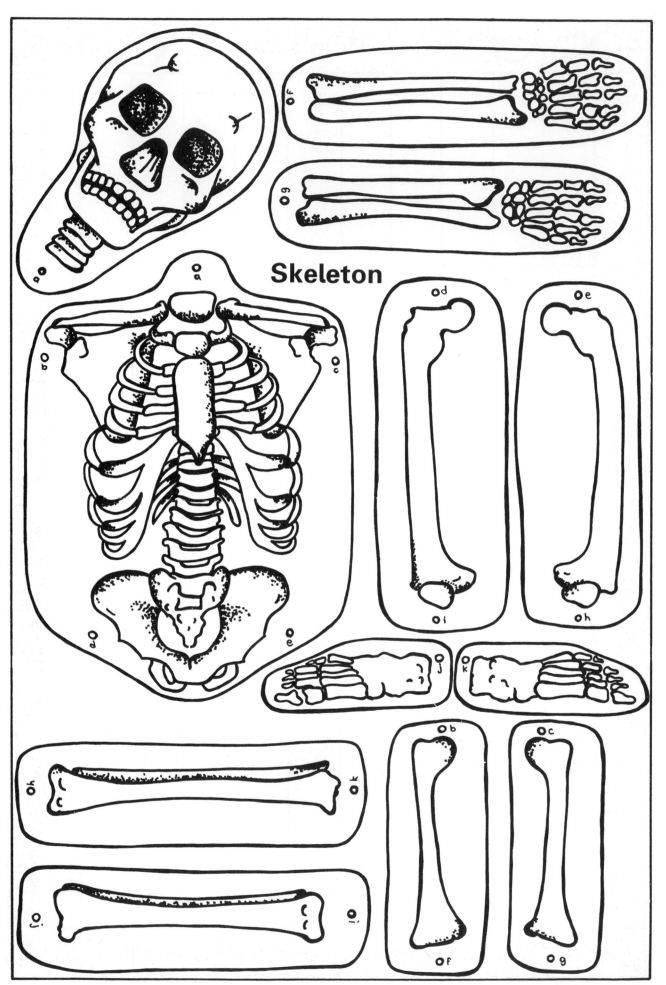

Skeleton

Draft sheet

The need:

Who needs it?

Draft design:

Materials needed:

Instructions for use:

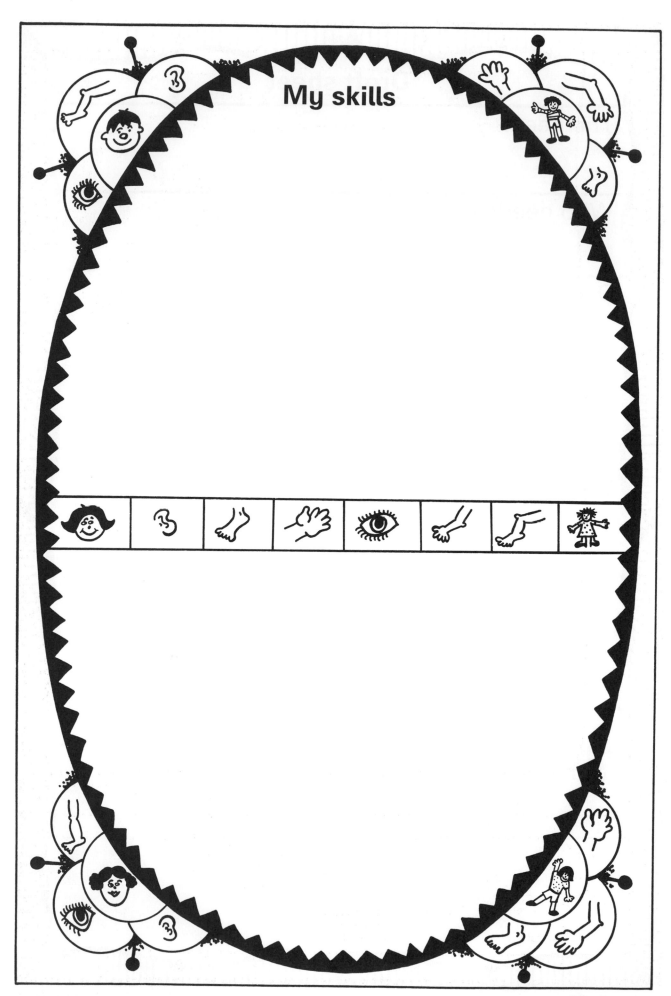

My skills

My design for a park

busy road

quiet road

key

trees

footpath

water

sand

bench

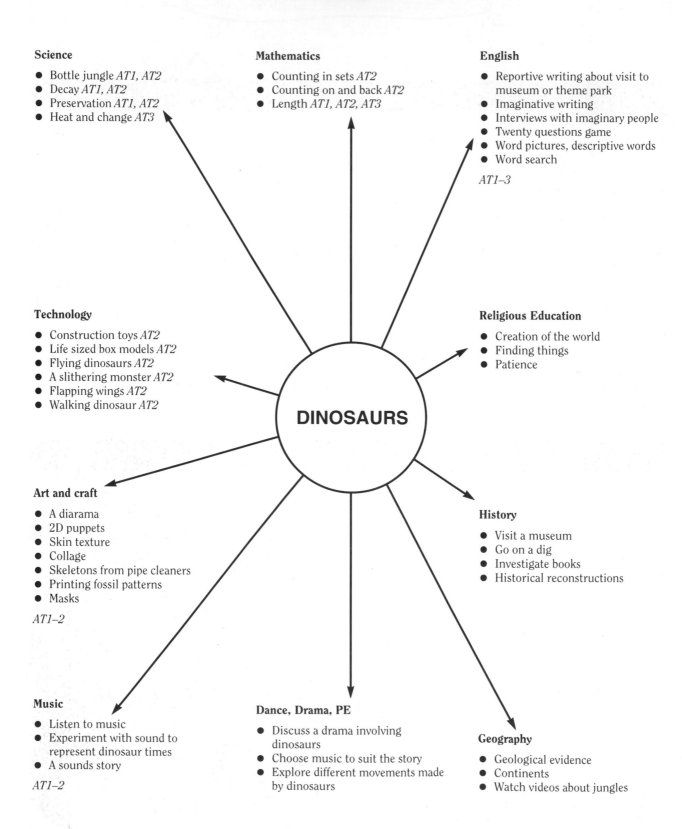

DINOSAURS

Science

- Bottle jungle *AT1, AT2*
- Decay *AT1, AT2*
- Preservation *AT1, AT2*
- Heat and change *AT3*

Mathematics

- Counting in sets *AT2*
- Counting on and back *AT2*
- Length *AT1, AT2, AT3*

English

- Reportive writing about visit to museum or theme park
- Imaginative writing
- Interviews with imaginary people
- Twenty questions game
- Word pictures, descriptive words
- Word search

AT1–3

Technology

- Construction toys *AT2*
- Life sized box models *AT2*
- Flying dinosaurs *AT2*
- A slithering monster *AT2*
- Flapping wings *AT2*
- Walking dinosaur *AT2*

Religious Education

- Creation of the world
- Finding things
- Patience

DINOSAURS

Art and craft

- A diarama
- 2D puppets
- Skin texture
- Collage
- Skeletons from pipe cleaners
- Printing fossil patterns
- Masks

AT1–2

History

- Visit a museum
- Go on a dig
- Investigate books
- Historical reconstructions

Music

- Listen to music
- Experiment with sound to represent dinosaur times
- A sounds story

AT1–2

Dance, Drama, PE

- Discuss a drama involving dinosaurs
- Choose music to suit the story
- Explore different movements made by dinosaurs

Geography

- Geological evidence
- Continents
- Watch videos about jungles

120

1 The dinosaurs were creatures that lived on earth 250 million years ago.

2 Some were carnivores and some were herbivores.

3 The world and its climate were very different then from the world we know today.

4 When they died, the plants and animals fell into different materials and were preserved.

5 We know that these plants and animals existed because we have found the evidence preserved in the form of fossils.

STARTING POINTS ▶

● Ask the children to bring in any model or toy dinosaurs they may have. They will probably have collections of books and posters too.

● There are several commercially produced videos on dinosaurs which are an excellent introduction to the topic. They show how evidence is collected, the worldwide sites, museum collections and very life-like animations of dinosaurs in scenes of the times. At the time of writing, Granada TV produce an excellent series of videos called *Dinosaur* with Walter Cronkite. Videos such as *The living planet*, and *Life on earth* show how we think the earth was formed and use footage of volcanoes and oceans to illustrate this. They also show animals which are alive today that look like their dinosaur ancestors, such as shrews, crocodiles, lizards. Walt Disney's *Fantasia* features Stravinsky's *Rite of spring* which is excellently portrayed as dinosaur times on earth.

● Visit a museum which has a fossil collection. Many museums now have model reconstructions of the development of life on earth and use diorama settings to help people understand what the world was like.

● Visit a fern house in a large botanical garden such as Kew, Southport or Tatton Park, to see what plant life was like in dinosaur times.

● Watch imaginative video stories such as: *Godzilla*, *The land that time forgot*, *The lost world*, and fun cartoons such as *The Nessies*. Stories of dragons are also of interest. Although not strictly relevant, they will at least serve to fire the imagination about monster-like animals.

● Visit a dinosaur theme park and see life-sized models in realistic settings.

ENGLISH ▶

Reportive writing

Get the children to write a factual account of a visit to a museum or a theme park. They can include details of how they felt as well as what they saw. Theme parks sometimes include sound effects which usually evoke a response from most children. Some parks also have a couple of dinosaurs for the children to climb on or kick, depending on the emotion they feel at the time! These models are actually very useful for the children to experience the huge sizes.

Imaginative writing

Ask the children to write imaginative pieces such as stories or short pieces of non-chronological writing. The following ideas might help get you started: a newspaper article about a shock discovery of a new type of dinosaur; a story of two very different dinosaurs who make friends; the discovery of a 2 m long bone in your garden; the story of the day you found giant reptilian footprints on the beach; the story of the night you camped on the shores of Loch Ness; a postcard from Dinosaur Island; an invitation to a dragon party; a list of things to take on a palaeontology expedition; a

spell to put out a dragon's fire; a poster showing how to dig fossils.

Interview

As exercises for Attainment Target 1, set up various interview situations. Work in small groups at first, and then let the class watch a series of interviews. For example, one child can act as a newspaper reporter or a TV reporter and interview another child who acts as one of the following: an explorer who has discovered a new land; a palaeontologist who has made a new discovery; a man who found a giant reptilian egg in his garden; a person who claims to have found a baby dragon.

They can plan the questions in groups.

Twenty questions

Again with Attainment Target 1 in mind, play this game with the class. Choose a panel of four experts which can be changed to give everyone a turn. The questions can relate to dinosaurs or to the world in general during their time. Let the children prepare questions in small groups first.

Word pictures

Try to build up not only a technical vocabulary but also a descriptive vocabulary based on this subject. Discuss some of the imaginative writing suggested above and have a brain-storming session, thinking of descriptive language. This need not be confined to the descriptions of the creatures themselves but can encompass human feelings about them in the various situations. For example, you may discuss fear, excitement, joy, disbelief, amazement, interest. Write words in related shapes as illustrated here.

Dinosaur pictures

122

Try to think up some descriptive phrases such as: giant-like; as big as a house; terrible and fearsome; swift as the wind; skin like a pebbled beach; terrible teeth.

The children can make short word pictures or blank verse based on one of the themes above. These can be written inside one of the dinosaur pictures on **Copymaster 6** (Dinosaur pictures). Enlarge the copymaster, cut out the pictures and let the children choose one to write in.

Word search

Take a dinosaur name such as 'brontosaurus' or 'tyrannosaurus' and see how many shorter words can be made from the starter word.

Copymasters

Use **Copymaster 1** (Cover sheet) as a cover for a topic book or for the children to do any of the pieces of writing on.

Use **Copymaster 2** (Dinosaur crossword) to aid spelling, search reading and memory. Discuss the answers first and write them on the board for the children to use as an aide-mémoire.

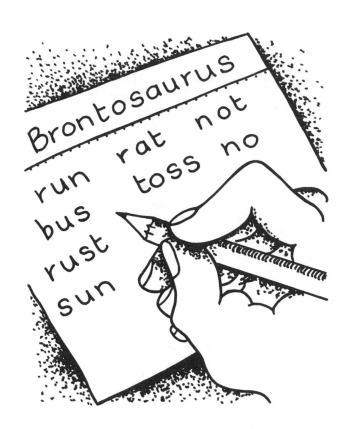

MATHEMATICS

Counting in sets

Practise counting in tens, fives, fours, threes and twos as part of your work on multiplication. Do this in verbal and written form. To make a link with the dinosaurs, see how many bipedal and quadrupedal dinosaurs you can identify. Some dinosaurs used their tail to aid balance just like a kangaroo does today, so this animal would represent sets of three. Thus use dinosaurs as the example when devising early multiplication problems. For example, count Diplodocus for sets of four, tyrannosaurus for sets of two, and so on.

Use sets to look very simply at the structure of geological time. Count in tens to see how a century is made, a thousand years and a million years. You can make up sets of tens using straws and red elastic bands, then band these into centuries with another colour and so on, just to give an idea of the vastness of a million years.

Counting on and back

To practise this ask the children to devise a simple board game using numbers to 20 in a number line.

When they are confident with the idea, make games going up in tens to 30, 40, 50, and so on. They can make up rules and forfeits with a partner.

If you are teaching numbers to 100, devise a type of snakes and ladders game based on dinosaurs. The snakes can be a Diplodocus' neck and the ladders can be a Stegosaurus' spine.

Use **Copymaster 3** (Search for the past) as a ready-made example of a board game. The players are palaeontologists on a dig, and the idea is to see what they can find on their expedition. As with real life expeditions, chance plays a part in how much they find.

Length

As part of your work on measuring length, look at the length of some of the dinosaurs and compare them to modern day creatures or things. Plot out the lengths of different dinosaurs on the playground using a trundle-wheel or metre sticks.

Use **Copymaster 4** (Comparisons) for the children to draw some modern things which are the same lengths as the dinosaur examples. It is important that they actually measure out the lengths to get the feel of the size involved.

123

Board game for counting on and back

SCIENCE

Make a jungle

Create a jungle environment such as once covered the earth. All you need do is make a bottle garden using a large carboy or old-fashioned goldfish bowl with the top sealed with cling film.

Put small plastic dinosaurs in between the plants so that you have made a Dinosaur World. Once the garden is set up, it should not need watering and the children will be able to see condensation forming on the glass and the 'rain' falling.

Decay

The dinosaurs and the plants in their world decayed, and the skeletons or imprints of the bodies have survived in petrified form. Attainment Target 2, 'Life and living processes' Level 2, looks at decay. Set up some simple experiments to observe this process.

1   Collect several types of waste, natural and man-made, and put them on display in the classroom to observe decay in air. Label them with their name and the date and see how long it takes for signs of decay to appear. Fruit and bread decay quickly.

2   Put a selection of waste products in water and watch as above to see if decay in water takes a different form.

Dinosaur world

124

3 Look for signs of natural decay. Go for a walk in the school grounds, the local neighbourhood or a woodland, and look for decaying leaves and grasses, fungi and moulds growing on dead wood, dead animals such as birds and decayed plant material in puddles and ponds.

Preservation

Peat-bogs
Look at the preserving properties of some materials such as peat. If you live near a peat-bog you may be able to find whole leaves and leaf skeletons preserved. Remember the recent find of 'Pete Marsh', an ancient man whose body was found preserved in a peat-bog. Pickled foods are preserved in a weak acid by the same basic method.

Drying
Natural materials can be preserved by drying all the water from them, for example dried flowers and grasses. Try drying flower-heads by the slow method of hanging them in a dry airy room. Examine some food stuffs which are preserved by drying.

Pressing
Pressing accelerates the drying process. Press some flower-heads and leaves to show how this works. The pressure from layers of rock helped to petrify the remains of skeletons.

Make plaster casts

Some footprints of dinosaurs have been preserved by a similar process. The footprints were made in soft mud which was then dried in the sun and the depression filled with sand and mud and eventually covered by rock deposit. The footprints are uncovered when such layers are split and exposed by quarrying.

To make casts of leaves such as ferns which grew in dinosaur times, press the leaves into a sheet of softened Plasticine® and remove carefully, leaving an imprint. Put a card collar round the imprint as shown, and fill this mould with plaster of Paris which has been mixed to a smooth consistency.

Let this dry thoroughly then remove collar and Plasticine® carefully to expose the raised impression. This can be rubbed over gently with shoe polish and then brushed to simulate coal. To get an idea of how the petrified footprints were actually formed, use a toy dinosaur to make footprints in the Plasticine® or in 'Newclay'.

Heat and change

The petrification process relies in part on heat and pressure, so look at how heat can change materials. Look at the materials needed to make biscuits. There are dry powders, fat and liquids, which when combined

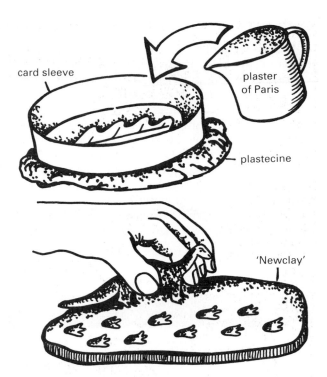

Make plaster and clay casts.

make a cold wet paste. When they are heated they become hard and change colour. Make dinosaur shaped biscuits to observe these changes.

Make a simple record sheet to record observations about changes in materials. Try heat and wax, cold and melted wax, heat and water, cold and water, uncooked pastry and heat, and plaster and water as for the plaster casts.

Changes

material	changed by	new material
melted wax	cold water	hard wax
water	heat	steam
sugar	water	sweet liquid
paper	fire	ash

125

Teeth and diet

Look at the teeth of modern animals that eat meat, or vegetation, or both. Pointed meat-eating teeth are designed for tearing and slicing flesh. Vegetable-eating teeth are designed to cut and grind vegetable material. Let the children have some experience of the different actions by cutting carrots with a knife and grinding some between two stones to simulate the action of the different teeth. You will also need to look at the teeth of different dinosaurs in pictures or by observing the skeletons. It was the shape of fossil teeth and the comparison with modern equivalents that gave early palaeontologists the clue to the dinosaurs' diet and so, life style. A meat-eater is usually a predator.

What did they eat?

TECHNOLOGY

Construction toys

Use Meccano®, Lego®, Duplo® and other construction toys to make dinosaur models. The children may come across problems of balance and stability of long limbs, depending upon which toy they use to construct their models.

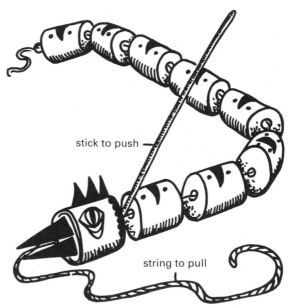

stick to push

string to pull

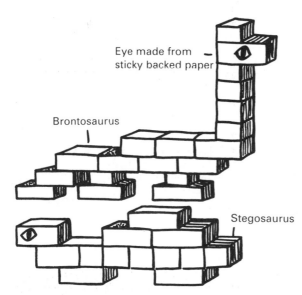

Eye made from sticky backed paper

Brontosaurus

Stegosaurus

A slithering monster

Make a fantasy dinosaur by connecting cotton-reels together in a long line. Discuss how they can be joined and still articulate. If you use string to join the reels, does there need to be a knot between each one? Can you use a stick or piece of string as a pull to make the creature move?

Life-sized box models

Try to make a life-sized model of a dinosaur or a fantasy monster using food boxes from the shops. Find out the actual size of the dinosaur first, and stack the boxes to calculate the number needed for the height, length, and so on. Discuss how to fix them together and how

to make the structure stable. Experiment with different materials for covering the boxes with 'skin'.

Flying dinosaurs

Make paper planes and decorate them with pens or crayons to look like skin or feathers (as for the early bird, archaeopteryx). A simple plane shape is shown here. Experiment with different designs to find the best glider.

Flapping wings

Make a flapping, flying dinosaur with a shape as shown, mounted on a stick or a rolled piece of paper. Let the children experiment with different wing lengths and shapes, and different types of folds on the wings. Decorate as a dinosaur or a bird. To make the creature fly, just wave the stick up and down with the wings held horizontally. You may use **Copymaster 5** (Flapping dinosaur) which is a template for a flapping dinosaur.

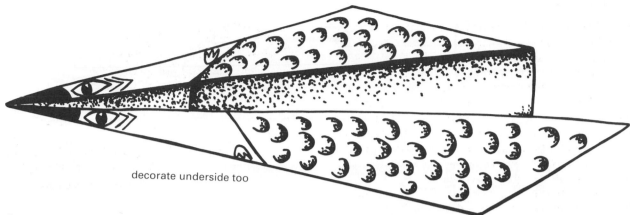

decorate underside too

Flying dinosaur

Walking dinosaur

Ask the children to draw a dinosaur body with two front 'arms' on one piece of card, and two large legs on another. Colour and cut out the drawings, then fix the

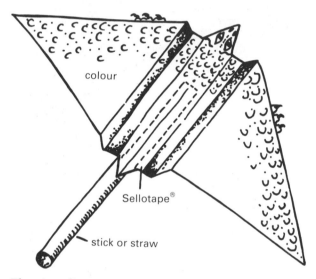

colour

Sellotape®

stick or straw

Flapping dinosaur

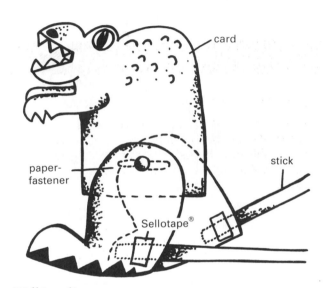

card

paper-fastener

stick

Sellotape®

Walking dinosaur

legs to the body as shown, attaching a stick to each leg to walk the 'puppet' along the table.

The body must not be too top heavy as it will fall forward, but you can leave this design feature to be experimented with.

ART AND CRAFT

A diorama

Get a large, shallow box or a shoe box, depending on how large you want the structure to be. Cut a piece of paper to fit across the two sides and the back of the box and decorate this as the background environment which can be jungle, desert, mountain range or swamp. Use paint, a collage of paper leaves or green cellophane® for water, or sprinkle sand on wet glue for desert or rough ground. Cover the outside of the box with paper or paint, then fit the decorated piece of paper inside as shown.

For the floor of the diorama use loose sand, crumpled tissue-paper, dry soil and real rocks and stones.

For the creatures use plastic model dinosaurs, drawings which have been cut out, Plasticine® or clay models. For flying creatures, fix short pieces of white cotton to cut-out pictures and attach the other end of the cotton to the inside roof of the box.

For under-sea dioramas, use Sellotape® to stick a sheet of green or blue cellophane® over the front of the box. Disguise the Sellotape® with a strip of activity paper glued over the join.

2D puppets

Make simple puppets by drawing a dinosaur (from a model or from a book) on to card. Colour and cut out

127

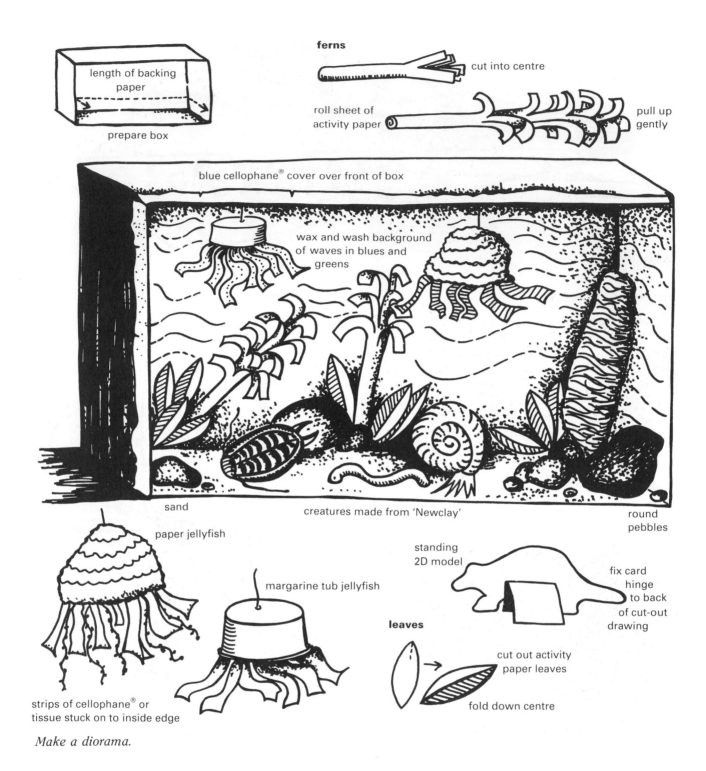

ferns

length of backing paper

prepare box

cut into centre

roll sheet of activity paper

pull up gently

blue cellophane® cover over front of box

wax and wash background of waves in blues and greens

sand

creatures made from 'Newclay'

round pebbles

paper jellyfish

margarine tub jellyfish

standing 2D model

fix card hinge to back of cut-out drawing

leaves

cut out activity paper leaves

fold down centre

strips of cellophane® or tissue stuck on to inside edge

Make a diorama.

the drawing, then fix a straw to its back. This is held to move the puppet. Use the diorama as a stage.

Skin texture

Look at present-day reptilian and amphibian skins, from the smooth skins of snakes to the gnarled skins of crocodiles and toads. Look at the shades of different colours on these skins and try to mix these in paint. Next thicken the paint with PVA glue, and use it to paint the skin patterns of the animals which have been observed. Try to recreate the texture of the skin using different implements to mark the thick paint. For example, you could use toothbrushes, glue spreaders,

paint-brushes, pieces of card, combs or old pencils. You can sprinkle sand or pulses into the wet paint for a very knobbly texture.

Collage

Jungle leaves

Make collages of jungle leaves using a variety of different textured fabrics and threads such as nets, brocades, thick hessians, felts, plastics, wools, and so on. Use threads of cotton, silk, string and wool to drape as tendrils and stems.

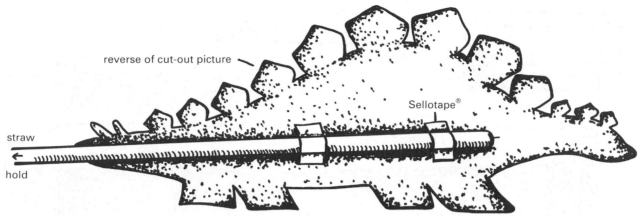

reverse of cut-out picture

Sellotape®

straw

hold

2D puppets

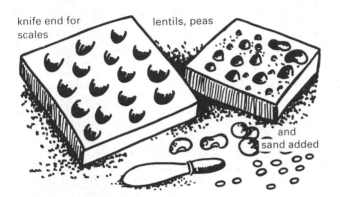

knife end for scales

lentils, peas

and sand added

Skin textures

Skeletons

Use pipe cleaners to make dinosaur skeletons. Stick them into a Plasticine® base. You will need to start off with the backbone and add long necks and tails to this. Wind pipe cleaners tightly round each other.

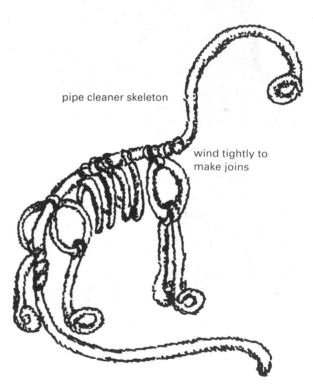

pipe cleaner skeleton

wind tightly to make joins

Collage

Dragons

Make collages of dragons using metal scraps such as old screws or nails, pull-can tops, bottle tops, milk bottle tops, strips of cooking foil. These can be individual pictures or collaborative efforts. Use heavy card, corrugated card, hardboard or plywood for the backing sheet to give strength and textural constrast.

Creatures

Make collages of creatures, such as the dragonfly, using stones, sand, shells and coloured fish-tank grit or glitter.

You can use combinations of materials to suggest different textures.

A dinosaur nest

Collect several halves of eggshell, wash and paint them in bright colours. Sit these in a nest of sand on a paper plate or old dish. To make newly hatched baby dinosaurs, use sausage shapes of Newclay or Plasticine®, and sit one in each eggshell.

Printing

Use thick string to make printing stamps and make abstract patterns with these. Look at the various shapes to be found in dinosaur times, such as linear patterns of ferns, spiralled trilobites, conical belamites, scales of skin, and translate these into the string

129

Dinosaur nest

Printing

Masks

patterns. Use thick paints to print with and try to find different surfaces inspired by the environment of the times. For example, use sandpaper for beach, plastic sheet or cellophane® for water, or brown paper for rock, and print designs on to these.

Make dragon, monster or dinosaur masks using sheets of paper, paper plates or shoe boxes as the base. Fix on to the top or the front of the head using a strip of card stapled on to each side. Decorate with paper sculpture or scrap features.

Masks

130

MUSIC

Listen

Listen to evocative music to help the children appreciate the quality of the creatures, their size, life style, the world around them and the vast periods of geological time. For example, *Thus spake Zarathustra* (the theme to *2001, A space odyssey*), Holst's *The planets*, Dvořák's *New world symphony*, and Saint-Saëns 'Fossils', from the *Carnival of the animals*. The latter is a xylophone piece which sounds like bones dancing.

Experiment with sound

Use a variety of instruments, real or home-made, to match sounds to different dinosaurs, weather conditions and earth movements. For example, use three or four bass notes on the piano for a brontosaurus, a trill on

the Swanee whistle for a pterodactyl landing, a scraping sound with the rickrack for a tyrannosaurus' teeth ripping meat. Let the children experiment to find sounds for creeping, leaping, volcanoes erupting, rain lashing down and the hot sun in the sky.

Sound story

Make a sound story using these sounds. First construct a simple story line and then match sounds to the events as they occur in chronological order. Some sounds may need to be present all the time, such as rain or wind. The children may also want to put in silences for dramatic effect, such as just before a predator attacks. Get them to agree on a start and a finish signal from a conductor. They can also write out a score for the players to read and they will need to think of symbols to represent the sounds.

A sound picture

DANCE, DRAMA, PE

Combine these disciplines together with the musical creation to produce a musical drama.

DANCE

Put the music, the movement and the story line together to make a short musical presentation. This might be a knight slaying a dragon, or a dinosaur protecting her young from a predator. Very simply, it could be a storm over a swamp with the children taking the parts of plants beaten down, water flowing and the wind blowing.

If they wish, they can use a recorded piece of music or indeed they can record their own composition on audio-tape so that the players are free to act too.

DRAMA

Put the children into groups and ask them to think of a simple story line involving dragons, monsters or dinosaurs. People can be included in this fantasy. They need to think of a place, one or more events, an opening and an ending. They can use the story line they used for music. Get them to work together to produce some of the actions in the story, for example a group could hold hands to become lava flow or a giant beast, or simply move at the same time to be a herd of animals. Ask them to include elements of aggression and flight in their story as these are part of dinosaur life. Recent evidence shows that some dinosaurs were good parents, protecting young, so this element could be included too.

PE

Explore various kinds of movement such as creeping, crawling, stepping, leaping (including taking off and landing). Try making different shapes and changing the size of the shape and its relationship to the ground.

Balance will be important in holding these shapes. Include time as an element and ask the children to find three different shapes and change from one to the other, holding each one for a specified time, such as the count of ten.

RELIGIOUS EDUCATION

There are several important themes which arise from a study of life so long past.

Creation

Creation is the major theme and you can find out more about how different religions view this, and discuss the many myths.

Finding things

Discuss the morality of keeping things we find. When does an article cease to be someone else's property and become a historical find? Do historical finds belong to the country they were found in? If you found a dinosaur skeleton, who would own it?

Patience

Palaeontologists require endless patience in their search for evidence and in uncovering bones embedded in rock. Set some shells in Polyfilla® and ask the children to remove them using a pin and a paint-brush. Talk about how they felt as they worked. Would they have felt any different if this was a real find? Would they be excited? You can also discuss endeavour. What makes the children try hard and persevere at a task? The story of Robert the Bruce and the spider makes a good illustration of this point.

HISTORY

Museums

Visit a museum and look at the real fossil finds. These can be drawn or photographed by the children so that the 'find' can be taken back to school to show that real palaeontologists record finds in this way. A notebook or record sheet of things of interest, or things you planned to see, can be noted on the trip.

Look at the type of evidence found to show that the dinosaurs existed. In the main, it is geological and fossil evidence with a great deal of educated guesswork based on the life styles of modern animals with similar body structures. With finds of life earlier than man, there is no pictorial or documentary evidence. However, such evidence does exist in the recorded findings of palaeontologists from the last century. The point must be made that this documentation is just another historical perspective.

Look at any skeletons of modern animals in the museum to help make comparisons.

Go on a dig

If you have any nearby sites of common geological finds, try to visit and organise a 'dig'. Collect small samples of rock and look for fossils. Carry small books to help identification on site as this will make the find more meaningful.

Sometimes small marine fossils can be found in surface limestone. Don't forget that photographic evidence of a find is preferable to demolishing a stone wall!

Look at the present state of knowledge

Collect books and pictures of dinosaurs and find as many different creatures as you can. Make an identification book with a picture of the dinosaur, its name and life style noted. Then when any child finds information about another dinosaur, he or she can add it to the file.

Using a geological time chart, try to sort any plastic models into their correct time period so that you know which dinosaurs were in existence at the same time.

You can also put them into sets of carnivorous, herbivorous or omnivorous animals. Remember to look at the teeth of any skeletons in the museum to find evidence of the eating habits.

Historical reconstructions

Use the pipe cleaner skeletons and Play-Doh® or Newclay to add body shape, just as palaeontologists do with real skeletons.

Use **Copymaster 6** (Dinosaur pictures) and **Copymaster 7** (Dinosaur world) which show a scene and a collection of dinosaurs that lived at the same time. Colour and cut out the dinosaurs, and stick them on the scene or let the children draw their own dinosaurs. The dinosaur pictures can be enlarged and used for language exercises or for technical vocabulary.

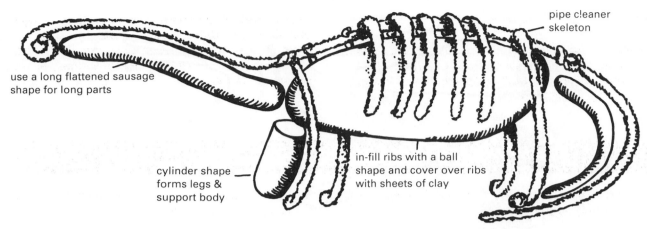

use a long flattened sausage shape for long parts

pipe cleaner skeleton

cylinder shape forms legs & support body

in-fill ribs with a ball shape and cover over ribs with sheets of clay

Reconstructions

GEOGRAPHY

Geological evidence

Collect samples of different types of rocks including limestone and coal. Look at the different properties and provide a sorting tray for the children to sort other samples into the correct sets.

Look at the world

Look at an atlas to see present day arrangements of continents, and compare this with reconstructed maps of the land mass in dinosaur times as this was quite different. Look in books to find where dinosaurs have been found in the world and you may note that the same dinosaur types are found on different landmasses because those landmasses have since moved.

Watch videos such as *The living planet* or any nature programme showing jungle, desert or mountain terrain.

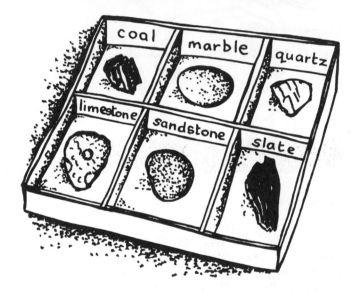

Dinosaurs 1

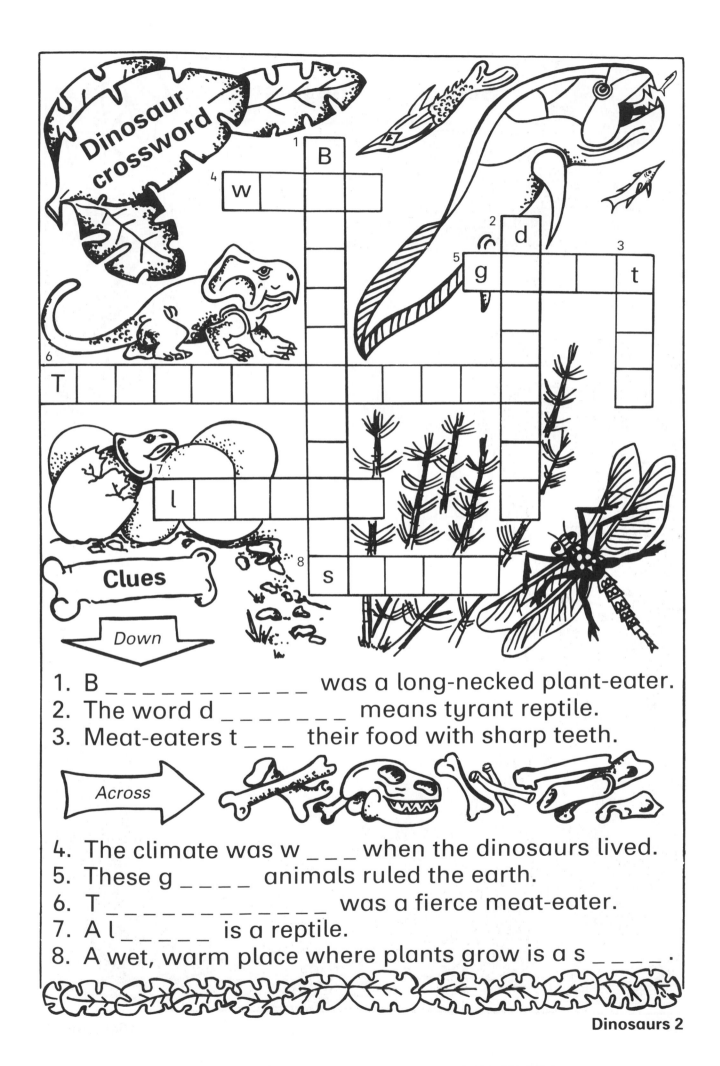

Dinosaur crossword

Clues

Down

1. B _ _ _ _ _ _ _ _ _ _ _ _ was a long-necked plant-eater.
2. The word d _ _ _ _ _ _ _ _ means tyrant reptile.
3. Meat-eaters t _ _ _ their food with sharp teeth.

Across

4. The climate was w _ _ _ when the dinosaurs lived.
5. These g _ _ _ _ animals ruled the earth.
6. T _ _ _ _ _ _ _ _ _ _ _ _ was a fierce meat-eater.
7. A l _ _ _ _ _ is a reptile.
8. A wet, warm place where plants grow is a s _ _ _ _ .

Dinosaurs 2

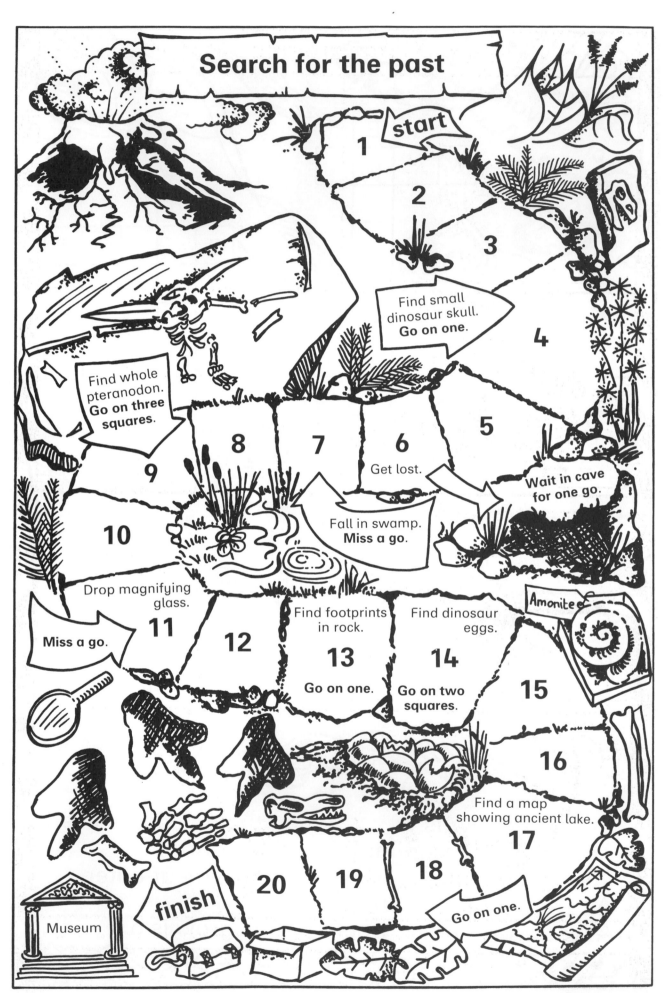

Search for the past

start

1
2
3

Find small dinosaur skull. **Go on one.**

4

Find whole pteranodon. **Go on three squares.**

8   7   6   5

Get lost.

Wait in cave for one go.

9

Fall in swamp. **Miss a go.**

10

Drop magnifying glass.

Miss a go.

11   12

Find footprints in rock.

13

Go on one.

Find dinosaur eggs.

14

Go on two squares.

Amonite

15

16

Find a map showing ancient lake.

17

Museum

finish   20   19   18

Go on one.

Dinosaurs 3

Comparisons

Deinonychus 4 m	
Triceratops 9 m	
Tyrannosaurus 15 m	
Diplodocus 30 m	

Find present day animals or things which are as long as these dinosaurs and draw them here.

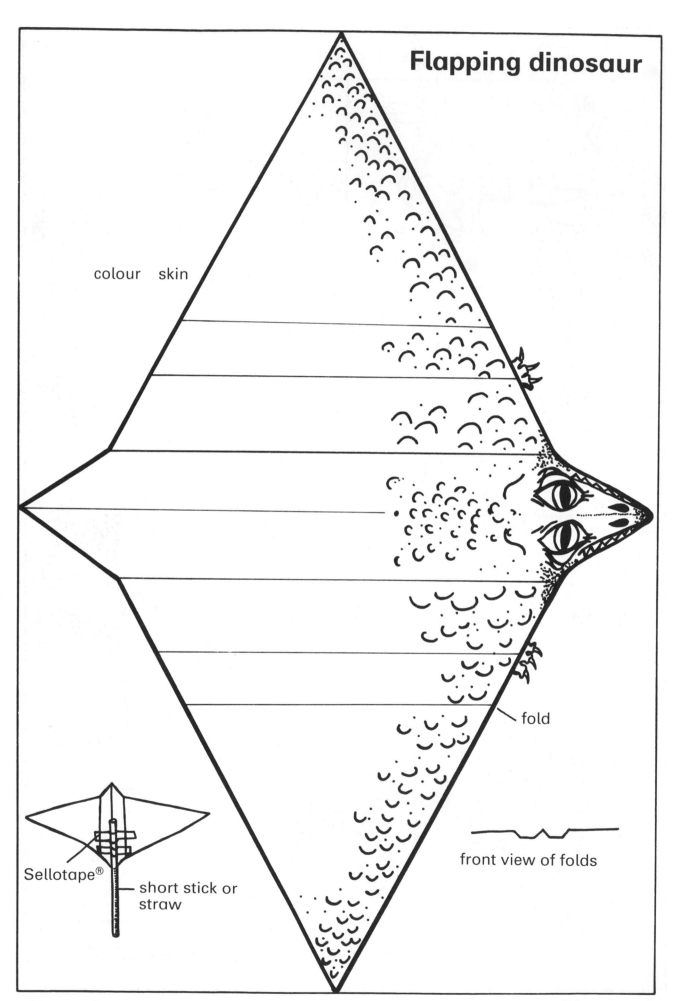

Flapping dinosaur

colour   skin

fold

front view of folds

Sellotape®

short stick or straw

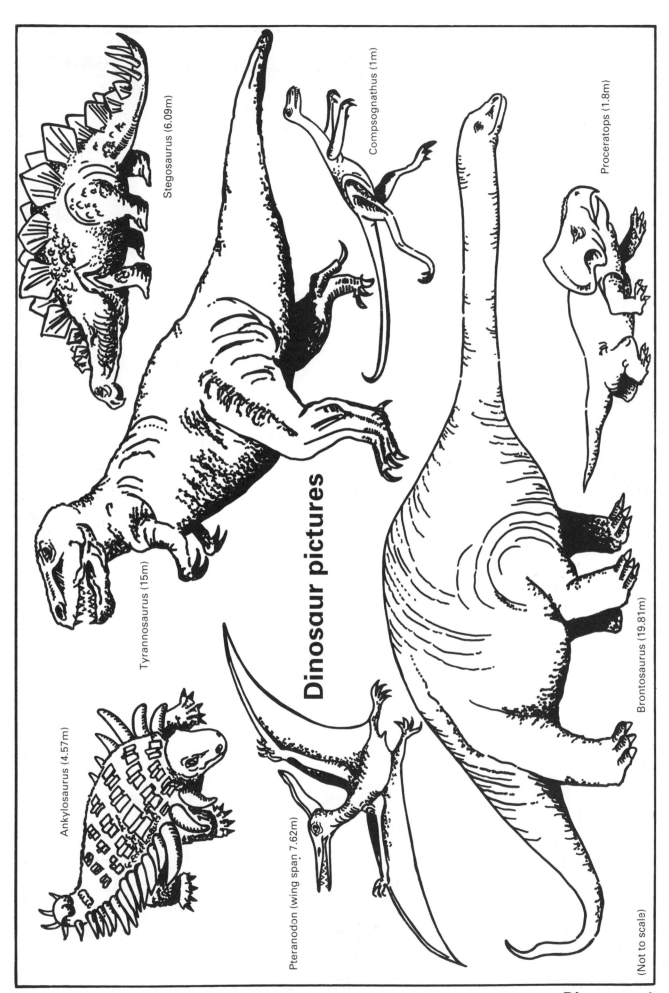

Dinosaur pictures

Stegosaurus (6.09m)

Compsognathus (1m)

Proceratops (1.8m)

Tyrannosaurus (15m)

Brontosaurus (19.81m)

Ankylosaurus (4.57m)

Pteranodon (wing span 7.62m)

(Not to scale)

Dinosaurs 6

Dinosaur world

FAMILY

English

- Looking at our families
- Relationships within family
- Writing about members of family
- Large class vocabulary sheet
- How parents help us, things we like to do with parents
- Animal families
- Imaginative writing – part of animal family
- Role-play centre – improvise domestic situation
- Reportive writing – trips to museums and large houses. Family gatherings and celebrations
- Family interests and hobbies *AT1–3*

Technology

- Design a house using construction toy *AT1*
- Planning interior of house *AT1*
- Design a pet's home *AT1*
- Homes of the future *AT1, AT2*
- Homes for different locations *AT1, AT2*
- Designing clothes for the family *AT1, AT2*
- Garden survey *AT1, AT2*

Art and Craft

- Paint family portraits
- Pictures of story book characters
- Families of colours, warm and cool
- Tones and shades of colour
- Vegetable printing, crayon rubbings, food dyes

AT1–2

Dance, Drama, PE

- The way different members of the family move
- Role-play centre for situations involving different members of the family
- Expressing emotions, families through history

Mathematics

- Sorting animals and plants into different families *AT1*
- Graphs of family size *AT4*
- Estimate and weigh amount of food they eat in a day *AT2, AT3*
- Pocket-money survey *AT2, AT3*

History

- Family tree
- Coat of arms
- Own family research
- Comparing family life
- Then and now
- Artefacts of family life

Science

- Animal families – camouflage *AT1*
- Communication – showing emotion *AT2*
- Family likeness *AT2*
- Growing processes of humans *AT2*
- School pets *AT2*
- Family food *AT2*

Music

- Families of instruments – brass, woodwind, strings, percussion
- Songs about the family

AT1–2

FAMILY

Religious Education

- Family of man
- Family friction
- Community spirit and good neighbours
- Comparing home life

Geography

- Street plan of area
- Where do members of a family live
- Types of houses – growth of village or town
- Cultural differences – family life
- Animal homes

1 Families usually consist of a mother, father and youngsters.

2 Families usually live together.

3 Parents look after the youngsters and provide food and shelter.

4 Parents teach the youngsters how to live.

5 The youngsters usually look like their parents.

6 Different cultures sometimes have different family systems.

7 There are different family structures to be found in this country.

STARTING POINTS

● Try to collect pictures of family groups, human and animal. Ask the children to bring in family group photographs, and create a display as the starting point. Collect pictures of the Royal Family, and make a display of these. Do not forget animal families and plant families. Collect posters and topic books with good illustrations and with a level of readability suitable for the children.

● Look for story-books with a strong family theme. Choose stories which illustrate good and strong family ties, and contrast these with others which show unkindness or cruelty on the part of one or other members of the family towards another. 'Cinderella' is a classic example of unfair treatment of this kind.

● Discuss families on television, such as those in favourite TV soap operas and comedies.

● Ask the children to bring in any toys such as Sylvanian Families so that they can sort them into family groups, and if you have a reading scheme and it has families as characters include them in your display as well. The *One, Two, Three and Away* scheme has the Red Hat, Blue Hat and Yellow Hat families, as well as

the Day family which can provide the cross-curricular link if required.

● As an extension of this topic, look at family homes for humans and for animals. There are many natural history videos available showing animal homes, and for human geography the children can look at homes in different countries. Look at the ways in which architects have designed buildings to fit in with local conditions today, and consider whether there are any elements of traditional construction or use of materials still being applied.

● Try to find out how homes have evolved through the ages, how use of available materials influenced how they were constructed, and ask the children to try and imagine what home and family life will be like in the future, contrasting this with a study of what home life was like for their parents and grandparents. Visit heritage museums which show how we used to live and look at the artefacts of bygone times. Places such as Beamish; Castle Museum, York; The Viking exhibition (Jarvik), also York; Wigan Pier; and Ironbridge, would all make interesting visits.

ENGLISH

Families

Set up the display of family pictures and topic books, and discuss with the children their views of their own family. Care and discretion will have to be exercised if you have any children in the class from one-parent families, or who are in the care of the local authority. Use discretion also when talking about relationships within individual families and keep the discussion general rather than specific. Encourage the children to write about the members of their family. Include poems and prose on the subjects of: My Mum; Helping Dad; My little brother or sister; Gran and Grandad.

Use **Copymaster 1** (Cover sheet) as a cover for the topic book, with a title written in the space. This sheet can be photocopied in two diagonally divided halves to make two sheets with room to write on. It can also be used for a poem or a piece of writing about the family.

See *Blueprints Writing* for other relevant copymasters, such as: My family, My house, Helping Mum or Dad, Going shopping, Bath time.

Make a large class vocabulary sheet so that the children can build up a bank of words for use during this topic. Get the children to paint large pictures of different members of the family, and cut these out and stick on to a large sheet of paper. Write the family words alongside the appropriate picture for quick and easy reference.

Discuss with the children the sorts of things their parents do to help them, and the sorts of thing they like to do with their parents. Also discuss the reasons why they should thank their parents for the things they do.

Talk about animal families. Let the children work in small groups to try to find out as much as possible about a particular animal family such as the cat family,

the insect family, the bird family, and so on. They can bring this investigation together as a presentation for the rest of the class to show what they have discovered.

Imaginative writing

As part of imaginative writing, the children can pretend to be members of a chosen animal family. Perhaps a baby bird in a nest, being fed by the adult birds with worms and insects, would be suitable. They could then write about the fears of learning to fly, and the ever-present danger of the cat. You can use the role-play centre to set up a home corner where the children can take on the role of any member of the family they wish. They can improvise their own domestic issues which they feel to be important and try to resolve them. Provide the children with a range of books which have strong family themes and discuss the behaviour of different members to each other. Talk about kindness and consideration, selfishness and cruelty.

Reportive writing

The children can do reportive writing about any trips they have made to museums or large houses. Try to ask an older member of the community to come into school to talk about family life when they were a child. The children can record their views as to whether they would have liked to have been a child then or not. Write about family gatherings such as birthdays, weddings, christenings, anniversaries or any other celebrations, and contrast the way different cultures enjoy family gatherings. Find out about the interests of other family members and make a magazine containing articles of interest. The children can carry out a simple survey among their own family members to decide what should be included. If any member of their family has a great interest or collection, they could come into school to talk about it to the children and they can then gather information for use in their article. Subjects might include computers, cars, flower arranging, gardening, cooking, handicrafts.

MATHEMATICS CM2

Sets and graphs

Cut out pictures of different animals and plants. The children can then sort these into sets of different families.

Make simple graphs of family size, showing families of three, four, five and more. As before, be sensitive to those children from one-parent families. The information can be displayed as illustrated overleaf.

Food consumption

The children can estimate and weigh the amount of food they eat in a day, and extend this further by trying to find out how much of a particular food is consumed by their entire family in one week. Keep the chosen food simple, and make sure the amount is capable of being measured easily. Bread might be a possibility, since the slices can be easily counted, or breakfast cereal which can be easily weighed. If the parents are agreeable, you could enlist their help in trying to find out their total weekly consumption of food. The school kitchens could also supply information about the amount of food and type of produce which goes to make the school dinners for a week. All this information could form the basis of a display to show how lucky we are in this country with the amount and variety of foods that are available to us, and contrast this with

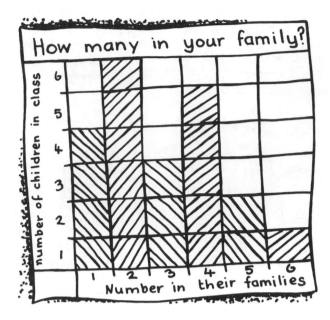

How many in your family?

Third World countries and Eastern European countries such as Romania and Albania, where the plight of the people, especially orphans, has been such a cause for concern recently. Such a contrast would be particularly suitable at Autumn time to coincide with the harvest-festival.

Pocket-money

If you think it appropriate, use **Copymaster 2** (My pocket-money) for the children to find out how they spend their pocket-money. Discuss with the children the amount they get, who gives it, and whether they have to do any jobs to earn it. They can fill in the form at home with the permission of parents, since this may be a sensitive area for some. Provided the information is forthcoming, the data can be presented in a visual form to show the most popular ways of earning the money, the most likely items bought with the money, and the average amount of money received.

SCIENCE

Animal families

Animal families can be highlighted by watching wild-life videos. Look at the habitat and location, look at the family groupings, and see whether the animals are solitary, live in colonies, or herd together. Try to find out about the role of the parents. Who does the hunting? Who protects? Who keeps watch? Try to identify whether the animal has any natural enemies and look at the ways in which the hierarchy is established and at the social interaction between other adults and families. Look at the life of the meerkats or prairie-dogs to find out whether the animals are gregarious.

Try to establish the importance of play as a factor in teaching the young to hunt and learn to be adults, and try to identify instinctive behaviour, linking this with the use of camouflage. The children could try to design a suitable background for a creature with a distinctive coat such as a zebra, giraffe, tiger or deer.

Communication in the family

Talk about emotions like happiness, sadness, joy, sorrow, anger, fear, and discuss ways in which we show these emotions. Is it always the face which is an indicator of how we feel? Try to get the children to think of all the different ways they can indicate how they feel, and consider what words they use to tell others what they are feeling. How does a baby let its mother know that it is hungry or tired?

Look at the way animals show emotions. Dogs are good examples. Discuss with the children what the following signs say about how a dog feels: wagging tail; baring of teeth; tail between legs, ears back and a crouched position with head down; tongue hanging out, panting, bright eyes, tail wagging and barking excitedly.

Use words such as menacing, scared, playful, happy and as many others as the children can think of to describe their dog. The children can also paint portraits of members of their family, showing the emotions of happiness, sadness, anger, surprise, fear and courage.

Family likeness

Use **Copymaster 3** (Family likeness) to fill in details of eye colour, skin colour, colour of hair and type of hair, e.g. straight, curly, wavy, spikey, thick, fine, wirey, long or short. The lower half of the sheet can be used to identify facial shapes. The children can fill in this sheet at home if desired. At the bottom of the sheet is an extra space for comments on similarities between different members of the family. Such things as sense of humour, likes and dislikes, abilities and skills, hobbies and interests can all be included. This is a data collection sheet, and the information can be used for comparison and the creation of group or class graphs. Try to encourage parents to send in photographs of themselves when they were the same age as their children and look for marked family characteristics.

From a study of similarities between parent and child, go on to look at differences. This is probably best done by examining those creatures whose young look nothing like the adult. Look at the life-cycles of a butterfly and a frog, for example.

Compare this with the life-cycle of the human. The children can sort and categorise pictures and photographs of humans at different stages of development: from being babies and young children, to teenagers and adolescents; from young men and women, to adulthood and middle-age; and finally to old-age and death.

School pets

If you have school pets, a male and a female, they may breed. Guinea-pigs, gerbils and rabbits are suitable, and the children can be encouraged to look after them during breeding time, making sure they have everything they need. (Remember DES regulations governing pets in schools.) The animals will need to be fed and watered and, once the babies have been born, care will be needed to make sure they are kept safe and warm. The children may well be encouraged to find out as much as possible about the needs of the particular animal, if they feel that they have the responsibility for their well-being. Remember with rabbits to keep the buck-rabbit well away from the little kittens, since they sometimes kill and eat their young. If you do not wish to go this far in your investigations and observations, perhaps one of the children whose dog or cat

has had young can be persuaded to bring them into school at a suitable time. One of their parents can also be present and talk to the rest of the class about the event. Include in your discussion collective nouns for groups of animals, such as a litter of puppies, a school of whales, a flight of eagles.

Crossword

Use **Copymaster 4** (Crossword) to identify the collective names used for the groups of animals shown.

Family food

Talk about the food which is eaten at home and the preferences of individual families. Do any families prefer a particular type of food, or is the food prepared in a special way? Invite parents from a variety of cultural backgrounds to talk about the food they eat and try some interesting recipes.

TECHNOLOGY

Design a house

Ask the children to design and build a house using one of the construction toys. The design can be sketched out on paper first of all, and then constructed. The 'house' can be for themselves, or maybe for the school pet. Alternatively, they can used cardboard boxes stuck or glued together to show the type of house they would like, and experiment with different materials to test for suitability. Encourage them to think of useful spaces and what goes into them.

As an extension of this type of work, the children may want to think about how families will live in the future. Discuss with them sources of energy, such as solar power and wind power, conservation, pollution and future modes of transport. Ask them to think about where the house of the future might be sited, for example underground, underwater, at the bottom of the sea, or on the moon. They can then be asked to think about the need to incorporate design features for the house which will overcome any problems associated with its location.

Ask the children to design clothes for different members of their family, especially if they do unusual jobs or have unusual hobbies or pastimes.

Garden design

Use **Copymaster 5** (Garden survey) to collect information about the kind of garden the children would like to have, and the kind of features they would like to see in it. They can ask other members of their family to say what they would like included, such things as a barbecue area, swimming pool, ornamental pond with fountain, vegetable plot, a sand-pit, play area with swings and a slide, a sheltered sunbathing area, a conservatory. The space at the bottom of the sheet is for the children to design a garden including all the features required by their family. They will need to think very carefully about how to site these features so that they do not, for example, have a child's sand-pit next to a deep swimming pool.

ART AND CRAFT

Family portraits

Paint family portraits. These can be done from memory or from old photographs. Encourage group paintings on a large scale.

Look at the families in the reading scheme, or in a favourite book or story, and paint pictures of these. Try to obtain some of the very stiff formal Victorian family portraits and contrast these with the more relaxed groups of today.

Families of colours

Look at warm colours and cool colours. Warm colours consist of red, pink, orange, yellow and brown. The cool colours are blue, green, purple and white. Create an abstract pattern by running a pencil over a sheet of paper. Make sure the spaces created are not too small, then paint in the different enclosed areas with warm colours. Try to ensure that no two adjoining spaces are painted the same colour. When the paint has dried, go

Family portraits

over the original pencil lines with a thick, gold marker pen. Repeat the process, this time using cool colours and go over the outline with a silver marker pen.

Make abstract patterns.

Tone pictures

Tone pictures can be created by choosing one warm or cool colour to paint a stripe diagonally across a sheet of paper. The differences in tone can be created by adding a little black paint to the original colour, to produce a darker tone, and a little white paint, to produce a lighter tone. For example, paint a diagonal solid red stripe, then add a very small amount of black paint. With this new paint mixture, paint a second stripe next to the first and, by adding a little more black paint each time, paint stripes across one half of the sheet until all of that side of the original coloured line is covered. To do the other side of paper, make sure the paint-brush is clean, and take some more of the original red colour.

This time add a little white paint so that a lighter tone is produced, and paint this lighter stripe of colour next to the original red stripe. Add a little more white, and paint another lighter stripe next to this. Repeat this, adding a little more white paint each time you paint a stripe, until the second side of the paper is covered. The sheet should now look like the picture illustrated below.

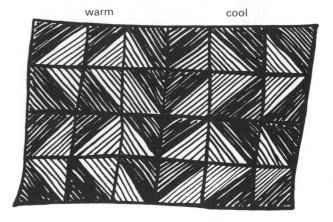

Tone pictures

Make two sets of sheets of warm colours and cool colours, and display them side by side to create a large abstract painting.

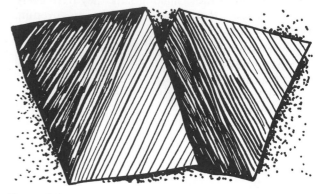

Vegetable printing

Bring in to school some of the fruits and vegetables used by the children's families, and use them to print patterns for wallpaper and fabrics for use in the home.

Vegetable prints

Cut the vegetables and fruit in half and dip in ink or paint-soaked sponges. This ensures a good application and helps to make a good print. Let the children experiment with sheets of paper folded into squares or rectangles inside which the children can print.

Crayon rubbings

Try to collect a selection of objects used by different members of the family, and do crayon rubbings of them. Firstly, place the objects underneath a flat sheet of paper, one at a time, and obtain an outline shape so that you can see where to rub. Then, by using the side of a thick crayon, rub gently over the whole surface of the outline until the pattern and shape of the object is revealed.

The objects used here might be the sort of things found in the kitchen, for example a string cloth, a spatula, scissors, knife and bread-board. A similar collection of objects can be collected from other parts of the house. Remember that flatter objects with a textured surface usually produce the best rubbings.

Food dyes

Many dyes can be obtained from the foods we eat, and tie-dyeing can be done using the natural dyes found in onion skins, blackberries, tea and coffee, saffron, beet-root, carrot skins and many more foodstuffs. Simply choose the food you wish to use, and boil the skins until the colour of the water is at the desired shade. The longer you leave it, the darker the colour will be. Make sure that you have enough raw material, as this also governs the intensity of colour. Add salt to fix the colour, and immerse the squares of cotton cloth for an all-over dye. For a pattern effect, wrap small stones in the cloth, twisting the cloth around them and tying with a waterproof string or thread. Leave this to soak in the dye, then take it out and open up to reveal a pattern.

Crayon rubbings

Tie-dying

MUSIC

Families of instruments

Look at the different families of instruments within an orchestra: brass, woodwind, strings, percussion, and encourage the children to listen to different pieces of music which feature a particular instrument or family of instruments. Benjamin Britten's, *Young person's guide to the orchestra* is ideal, and takes the listener through each section of instruments.

Set up a music corner and highlight a different family of instruments each week or fortnight. Display pictures of the featured instruments and, if possible,

also include some real instruments for the children to handle. Have a tape recorder and headphones, and supply tapes of music featuring the instruments on display, so that the children can listen and become familiar with the sounds made by the different families of instruments.

Sing songs

Look for songs to sing with a family theme, such as: 'Family of man'; 'Oh my Papa'; 'Mother of mine'; 'Grandad'; 'Sisters'; 'My brother'; 'Grandfather's clock'.

DANCE, DRAMA AND PE

DANCE

Talk about the various members of a family, and ask the children to think about the different ways in which

they would move. For example, young babies crawling and toddling about; children skipping, jumping and running; teenagers skateboarding and being cool; grandparents and old people not quite so fast as before,

147

and some having great difficulty to walk at all. Let the children try to move in these ways, accompanied by a piece of music or an instrument to suggest a particular way of moving.

DRAMA

Use the role-play centre to act out situations involving different members of the family. Set up a shop so that the situations can be developed, for example quarrels between neighbours, and different families helping each other in times of difficulty. Try to encourage as many different situations as posible, to enable the children to express a variety of different emotions. These situations can also be set at different times in the past or in the future, and the children will have fun collecting or designing suitable artefacts to give a sense of realism.

Act out situations set in the past.

RELIGIOUS EDUCATION

Family conflicts

Think about the family of man, and talk about consideration for others, caring and sharing. Ask the children to try and identify situations which may cause upset in their own family, for example arguments over which programme to watch on television, being asked to run errands, or doing jobs around the house like tidying rooms or washing up. What is it that causes conflict? Go on to develop this theme by trying to find out what can cause conflict in the wider community or neighbourhood, and consider what we can do to ease the tension. Stress that we are all equal, and note that Christ instructs us to, 'Love thy neighbour'. You should also consider what other religions have to say about how we can live together in closer harmony.

Tension can often arise because we feel threatened. When you get to know someone, that tension is often relieved. Try to build bridges between different groups of people by finding out how they live and what they believe in. Look for areas of common ground. Look at special family occasions and the ways people celebrate. Look at home life and invite people in to talk about the way they live, and try to find out about each other's festivals. In this way we can try to get to know more about each other and come to realise that despite outward appearances, we really are just the same in lots of ways.

HISTORY

Family tree

Use **Copymaster 6** (Family tree) for the children to chart their own family tree back to their grandparents. The children can gather the information at home then fill in the sheet at school.

Family names

Ask the children to think about their family name, and try to create a family shield to illustrate it. Certain names will lend themselves immediately to this, such as Wood, Hill, Smith. Others will need a little more

Family shields

imagination but all children, perhaps with a little help, should be able to make a shield of some kind.

Family research

Ask the children to try and find out where their grandparents lived as children, and compare the type of houses they grew up in, with the houses we have now. What do we have in our houses that they did not? How did they heat their homes? How did they wash their clothes? How did they dress? Invite grandparents into school to talk about their early lives. Take the children

to one of the many heritage centres to investigate even further into the past, to see how Victorian families used to live. Some National Trust properties have an educational facility which allows the children to dress in period costume and experience a day in the life of a large house.

Make collections of old artefacts and utensils, and make a display comparing them with the gadgets we use today. Choose a period in history and compare family life then with family life now. Look at cartoons of the Flintstones and the Jetsons, and compare the Stone Age with the space age.

GEOGRAPHY

Where we live

Try to obtain a large-scale street plan of your area or, if possible, take the children out and draw your own. Using this, they can mark on areas of different land use and identify main buildings. This could form part of a large class display with each of the children writing their name on the house they live in. Each child could also mark on their route to school.

Look at house types in your area. Identify terraced, semi-detached, detached, low-rise or high-rise flats, and other types such as farms and cottages. Look for the areas, especially in older villages, where the oldest houses are situated. These can often be identified by datestones or the style of building. Look also for the newer developments, and try to find old maps of the area to see how it has grown. See if any families have lived in the area for a long time. Look in the local churchyard for clues, and ask the children to find out if most of their family live close to each other, or if they are all scattered about in different towns and villages, or even in different parts of the country.

When you have studied the plan of the area in which you live, use **Copymaster 7** (Where we live) for the children to try and think of ways in which their area might be improved. They may want to provide some of the amenities shown at the bottom of the sheet, and this may mean that some property in the area will have to be removed in order to create space for them. Discuss with the children the sorts of changes they would make, and the reasons for their changes. If property had to be removed, where would it be relocated? What effects might the changes have on the people affected?

Look at cultural differences between families of different ethnic backgrounds. Invite people from the community to talk about family life in their country of origin. Talk about food and clothes, and look at house types and conditions. You could make a world map to show how climatic conditions can determine the design and the materials from which the house was made. A look at animal homes can also be included at this point if required.

Family 1

My pocket-money

Name	Date

1. Who gives you the money? _____
2. When do you get it? _____
3. How much do you get? _____
4. Do you do any jobs in return? _____

5. How do you spend the money?

_____   _____ p

_____   _____ p

_____   _____ p

_____   _____ p

_____   _____ p

_____   _____ p

_____   _____ p

total   _____ p

6. Do you always buy the same things?

7. Do you save any money?

8. Do you think you should get more money?

Fill in one of these sheets each week, for three weeks, to compare how you spend your money.

Family likeness

	mother	father	me	brother	sister	others		
eyes								
skin								
hair colour								
hair type								

face shape	mother	father	me	brother	sister	others		

Other similarities, e.g. sense of humour, likes and dislikes.	

Family 3

Family crossword

Clues

Across

2. A g _ _ _ _ _ _ of geese.
4. A p _ _ _ _ of lions.
6. A s _ _ _ _ _ _ of whales.

Down

1. A s _ _ _ _ _ of fish.
3. A l _ _ _ _ _ _ of puppies.
5. A n _ _ _ of ants.
7. A h _ _ _ _ of cows.
8. A f _ _ _ _ of sheep.

Garden survey

What things would you like most in the garden?

Mother	
Father	
Sister(s)	
Brother(s)	
Other family members	
Pet	

Now plan a garden for your family containing all the things they want.

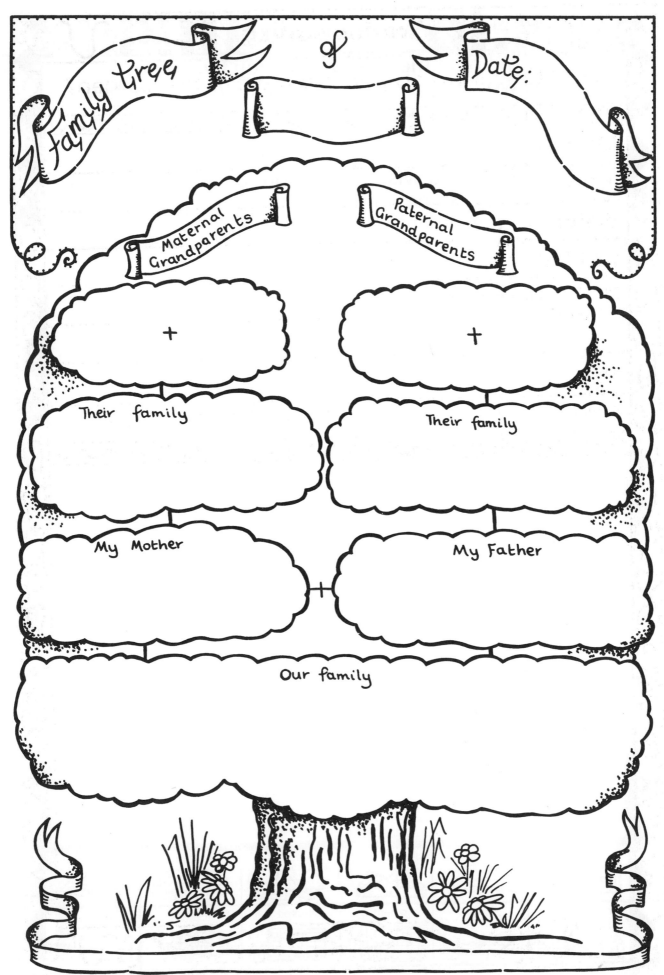

Family tree of

Date:

Maternal Grandparents

Paternal Grandparents

+

+

Their family

Their family

My Mother

My Father

Our family

Family 6

Where we live

If you could plan the area where you live, what facilities would you include? Imagine you have been asked to plan a whole town. Discuss with a partner where you would site all the things needed, then draw a plan of your ideal town in the space below. Remember, if you wish, to include roads, motorways and railways. Some amenities are shown at the bottom of the sheet to help you.

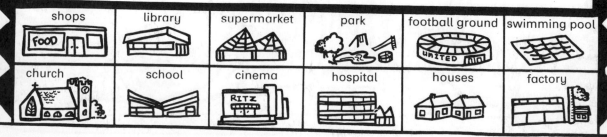

| shops | library | supermarket | park | football ground | swimming pool |
| church | school | cinema | hospital | houses | factory |